Ritchie,
my long-time
very special friend~
Love,
Stephie

*I*nterrupted *L*ives

 Stephanie M. Krulik

Stephanie M. Krulik
6/12

MIDDLE
RIVER
PRESS

ISBN 978-0-9846071-3-6

Interrupted Lives
Published by Middle River Press
1498 NE 30th Court
Oakland Park, FL 33334
middleriverpress.com
First Printing — Printed in the USA

This is a Holocaust survival story.

It is the linked experiences of two people,
who became one person to survive.

For my family
Gary, Doug, Tracy, Holly, Tom,
Sydney, Joshua,
always...

ONE

I do not know of any word in the Hebrew language more important than the word Zachor, *which means "remember," and the admonition, "do not forget."*

— *Gerd*

I AM SO TIRED. I am so tired of that swish-click sound I hear night after night, night after charcoal night, as I double lock our heavy front door, after I already have double-locked the door of our screened-in aluminum enclosure, which keeps us safe inside this concrete and stone condominium. I fear the old shuffle-slush, shuffle-slush steps, which closely follow me as I move around here day after day, night after night, are the dark shadows of my other life.

My other life began in a world far away from here. It was a contaminated world, a humiliating world. It was a world that haunts me still.

Tonight, my tan leather slippers shuffle-slush into our warm white kitchen. My nose tingles and my mouth waters from the lingering aroma of Inge's newly boiled chicken soup; from the rich dark flanken meat nestled next to the small, white potatoes and the sweet, orange baby carrots, simmering on the stove in the worn aluminum pot; and from the cinnamon-speckled apples baking in the oven.

So what if I cannot sleep? That is nothing new. So what if my pounding head won't leave me alone? That is nothing new, either. It seems like I already have lived two lifetimes. I can see my young self slithering around like a slippery eel. I would have lived in dense, dark water and would have hidden myself behind a black, jagged rock. But then, the easy path was not mine to take.

So, I go to the sink, open the tap, and patiently listen to the sound of that cool running water as it trickles out like a brook, bubbling down into a lush, green valley below. Ah, ah, I remind myself: here I am taking a sip of life.

But, it is that life and that time that always keeps me awake. My watering eyes gaze into the surrounding night. I remember a time, it was 1933, yes, and it was seventy-six years ago when I was a child and lived in the center of Berlin, when the sky was darkened always with dense, black clouds and the air hung like thickened mold.

My family, my father, Lewek, and my mother, Frieda, and my sisters, Eva and Rosa, and I lived in a large, red-brick flat-top apartment building with the address of Muenz Strasse 14+16. The address changed many times. At first it was called Muenz Strasse 25, located at the corner of Dragoner Strasse, the so-called _Scheunenviertel,_ a predominantly Jewish and a mostly Eastern Orthodox enclave. Our building and the one directly next door was large enough to house the renowned watch store Brandmann.

Over the years, those two buildings would house the famous and the infamous. They would stand at the threshold of all of my beginnings and some of my almost unbelievable endings.

I clearly remember a time, another time and another place, when I am standing with a small group of young men, against a wall built upon a darkened street, the pavement looming in front of me. I look down that street, and I see a young Jewish woman quickly walking and carrying her precious brown-haired, brown-eyed little girl on her arm. I think the little one is about three years old, and I could tell she was frightened; she was cold but mostly hungry. I see the *Schutzstaffel*, the German SS officer, his pristine, black leather boots pounding, pounding as he nears.

"Halt! Halt!" he screams. Saliva drips from his mouth. His upper lip curls around like a rattlesnake ready to strike. "*Halt!* What are you doing out here? You miserable sniveling Jew! Shut that girl up! Shut that dirty little thing up!"

His whole body contorts, he sneers at them, showing his densely packed yellow teeth. "Shut up! Shut up! Shut up!" He rips the little girl out of her mother's arms.

The gunshot echoed and echoed and echoed.

I can still hear the mother screaming out her daughter's name, "Shulamit! Shulamit! Shulamit!" just before the Nazi SS officer turns his gun on her.

I think I am going to throw up. I am dizzy. The burning fire is again in my head. I trip as I try to steady myself against the cold kitchen sink.

"Gerd, Gerd, are you all right? Are you all right? Come

back to bed. Come to bed now!" my Inge calls. My sweet Inge calls me back to her side.

Inge won't come out of our safe bedroom. I am glad it is not her tonight. I am glad the thoughts and the searing aching pain are mine alone.

Two

When you know your parents are hungry, you try to get some food for them — no matter how.

—Gerd

THE MORNING SUN shines through our bedroom window, arousing us, encouraging us to begin our day. My headache has left me as eagerly as it began. Inge has fixed us a breakfast of poached eggs and buttered rye toast. I wince when I see that her delicate hands still shake as she pours hot coffee into our cups. One sugar cube rests on the bottom.

I look out the breakfast room window and see a briskly swaying palm tree steadying itself against the humid Florida wind. "*Ja. Ja*, this is a good breakfast, Inge," I say. She smiles. If I look closer, the top of the palm tree disappears, and I again can see the patchy brown, rough fields and springtime green leaves of so many other trees reaching up to that gray, German sky.

I came to the Farm, this new agricultural village called Neuendorf, on April 1, 1940. I laugh to myself when I tell people Inge must have heard about me. I like to think she must have come looking for me when she arrived two months later on June 17. I see that Inge's hair falls in soft dark-brown curls to her shoulders. Her skin is pure and unblemished. When she looks at me, all I can see are the great round discs of her intelligent brown eyes. The corners of her mouth turn up when she speaks:

"*Guten Tag. Mein name ist Inge Franke. Ich bin von* — I am from Herne in Westphalia." she says.

"*Guten Tag. Mein name ist Gerd Bocian. Ich bin von Berlin.* I am 17 years old." I answer.

"I am also 17," Inge says sweetly. "I am new here. I already know a few girls, but you are the first boy I am talking to." She bends her head down and murmurs, "I think you are nice."

I think she is nice, too. There is something about her that makes me want to bring her into my life. I know this already. I find myself talking quickly and easily to her. "Inge, we have come to a very nice place. Here we are today, just two people of so many. I am one of the ninety boys who live here, and you are one of sixty girls. We have all come to work this land and get to know our Germany. I am eager to learn how to farm and tend the animals. I think you will like it here, too. I have seen that the girls do different work here, but it is all for a good purpose. I think our new home could be our path to Palestine. Inge, I have great hopes for the future. I am proud to tell you that I am a Zionist."

Inge looks directly at me. Perhaps she likes what I am saying. Her questioning mind is like a supple sponge, wanting always to absorb more. I am happy to tell her all I know about our new home. "Inge, come here. I would like you to know about this farm. We are now living almost fifty kilometers east of Berlin. We are surrounded by the dense Brandenburg countryside. This farm has been owned by a wealthy German Jew by the name of Miller since 1916. He is a brilliant man. I heard that he could read the Nazi mind." Inge's bright eyes open even further. I believe she looks dazed and at peace. I take her hand, and I feel my heart skip a beat. I shudder a little.

"Inge, be careful," I say. "The Gestapo is not far away. This man Miller knows about this — he knows we are in a peculiar situation here, but for now, we are probably safe." Inge squeezes my hand a little tighter. "Gerd, I understand what you are telling me. You make me feel safe."

Miller does want us safe. I have made my home on this land. Here I learn about agriculture. I march in a big group out into the surrounding dense forests every day. I can feel the heat of the bright afternoon sun baking down on my back. I learn to plow the newly planted string beans, carrots and corn. I can see the cabbages grow strong and wide and watch the potatoes peek out of the newly toiled, rich brown soil. I learn how to pull and clean the vegetables and carry them inside, so the girls can make soup for our dinner.

"This is good, Inge," I tell her again. "Now, if we work hard in this place, we could even get a diploma. Inge, you are lucky to be here. Really, we could be much, much worse."

For a while, there were too many of us to work only on the farm. Some of the boys work outside the farm, in other fields, but we are all working for the war effort. I am trusted. I am lucky; I am able to get a pass to go home on some weekends. I am scared on those dirt roads, but I want to see my family. I cram my coat pockets with the extra potatoes and carrots I saved all week. When you know your parents are hungry, you try to get some food for them — no matter how. I know it is a dangerous time, but my life is better on this farm.

The farm helps me pay attention to my life. I watch Miller, and I listen carefully to his instructions, as if I am back in school. I learn more about farming; I watch everything around me. I see that once a month comes this man, Ferdinand Weber, this German Jew, a fat Nazi with the golden button on his uniform. He goes off to the barns to see the hundreds of cows. He is here to test the fat content in the milk. It doesn't take long for Miller to ask him to take charge of the farm. Ha. Now, the Gestapo is happy; one of their own could watch over us. This is good. Now I think maybe we really are protected.

I am sure Weber likes me. One chilly, overcast morning when we are standing in line, waiting for our daily instructions, he pulls me out of the line and walks quickly with me to the chicken hatchery. Every day from then on, I stuff my hands into the dusty feed bags and wave my arms like a magician with a wand, spreading feed to 2,000 chickens. The smell is like breathing in soggy, rotten eggs.

"*Oy,* what am I up to? From this I will get a diploma?" I chuckle to myself. Probably I think too much.

I learn right away that this farm is one of the best new places like this in Germany. On the first day I arrive, I walk up from the dusty gravel road, and I see the roomy, three-story, gray-green brick manor house and surrounding two-story out buildings just sitting there staring back at me. The place looks like a richly colored painting with the buildings set on hundreds of wooded, grassy acres. This is good, I say to myself. The farm gives me a good place to live and to work. I didn't want formal school anyway.

Ja, I am proud that my early schooling was in a *cheder,* a religious school. I am proud that I graduated from the Jewish High School in Berlin for boys only, a famous school founded by Moses Mendelssohn, the great privileged and protected German-Jewish philosopher, whose ideas became like my own. Later, I would realize Mendelssohn's ideas of religion and their effect on human behavior would have a dramatic place in my salvation.

Although they never really bother me or my friends when we are at school, the Hitler Youth, with their knee-high pants, tan shirts and ready right-arm salute, make me uncomfortable. Every day, it seems that the air is always dense with fog and black dust. Every day, Hitler is already on the march. I hear unbelievable whispers that this man, Hitler, one day will exterminate all the European Jews.

I am here for a few more months. I have many friends, but not like my friendship with Inge. One early afternoon while we are resting on the soft summer grass, Inge touches my arm and says, "Gerd, I want to tell you about my family. I want to tell you about my life before I came here." Inge settles herself comfortably before she says, "My father, Solomon, and my mother, Alice, used to be very wealthy. My mother's cousin was the Baroness Rothschild. Really, Gerd, I am telling you the truth. My mother always wore her diamonds and rubies with pride. My parents indulged me, Gerd. They used to buy me pretty clothes and expensive jewelry. I know they love me very much. We had servants, Gerd, who took care of our house. They took care of me. I have an older brother, Henry; he spoils me, too. My grandfather, the first Jew in my hometown, who made a study of our little town, hugs me and loves me so much."

"You are lucky, Inge. To come from such a family like this, to have a mother and father who devote themselves to you. I am happy for you. I can tell you that my two sisters and I were treated also with love and respect. I have a wonderful family. Now, Inge, I am listening. Tell me more."

"I went to school in a girls *Gymnasium*, but I only made one good friend, she says. "We were the only two Jewish girls in the school. When this friend left one night to go underground with her parents, I left school, too. I was afraid. I told my parents I would not go back there, not even to pick up my diploma."

"Inge, you are not alone. I, too, know that something is happening. Something is happening all over Germany. Something is happening above us in the uncertain German sky. Each time I go to Berlin to see my parents, I see Jewish people everywhere standing in small groups; the elders whisper and the rabbis gesture. I see men hiding in blackened doorways. I don't see too many people on the streets anymore. Window shades are drawn even in the daytime." Inge nods and waits for the rest of my story.

"It was awkward for me when my parents never spoke to us about this; they sat on our well-worn couch in our comfortable living room. They silently took pieces of newspaper and carefully wrapped a silver menorah. They took more newspaper, tore it in little pieces, and put family trinkets safely away. Some of our books I believe I will never see again."

Inge nods again. "My family lived like this, too, Gerd. My mother and father knew they have to save their prize possessions, or they may not ever see them again. I still see my mother with tears in her eyes, rolling her gold jewelry in a ball of wool and placing it carefully in a container that would soon be taken safely out of Germany. My father told her not to pack any furnishings, just her most valuable possessions. One day this truck comes, and men put our bulky container in the back. They take it to a ship sailing from Rotterdam to America.

"We were excited about getting away, going to this safe country where we would all be together. But. Gerd, something terrible happened. We thought Holland was a safe place, and then the bombs came — the bombs fell everywhere. Our big container blew up into little pieces. We had nothing.

"Gerd, in early January my father arranged a visa for the family to go to Paraguay. Very quickly we packed some clothes, some warm sweaters, a blanket, some food, and in the middle of one night, we walked out. When we came to the border between Germany and Holland, the Dutch border guards searched us and shouted, "This is a fake. This is a fake! This visa is a fake!" The words, 'Not admitted to Holland,' are embedded in my mind."

I shudder. I cannot believe what I am hearing. "How terrible, Inge. How terrible to have this happen to you and your family. Nothing is predictable anymore. Now, Inge, tell me more."

"We had to wait, Gerd. We wait, and we wait. For a little while, we stay with my aunt and uncle. Some of our non-Jewish neighbors want to take us in, but my parents were very proud people. They always answer *no*.

"Then in February, my father comes hurrying home, shouting for all of us to come to him. He got visas to go to Panama, but he only had enough money for himself, my mother, and my uncle. It was easier to get the visa for my uncle; the Germans are happy to have another man leave.

"First, they go by train to Italy. Then, they could embark on a ship in Genoa. 'Henry and you will come after,' they promised. They *promised*. I know this wasn't their fault. We stayed in Germany at my aunt's house, the house of my mother's sister.

"I stayed there for two months. I missed my parents terribly. I didn't want to stay with my aunt anymore. Henry is my older brother. He stayed.

"One day, my aunt wore her coat with the ugly yellow Jewish star and walked by the city walls covered with the words, 'Dirty Jews.' She kept her head down and her eyes on the road. She went directly to the Jewish Community Center and asked permission for me to go to this farm.

"I came to the farm. Gerd, I won't put any food in my mouth."

"Inge, Inge, what are you telling me? You won't eat? Why won't you eat? "

"Gerd, I can't look at these old metal plates and bowls. I can't touch the metal forks and spoons. My head gets dizzy. In my home, we sat at a polished wood table set with an embroidered linen tablecloth; we ate from the finest china. We drank from cut crystal glassware. Even when we had to let our maid go Henry and I willingly helped our mother.I don't know what to do. I am getting weaker, and I cry so much, and I don't seem to care."

"I will help you, Inge. I will make you better. Together we will make you better."

THREE

*After all, this is not Poland or Russia. This is a
civilized country I am living in. Pogroms do not
happen here.*

—Gerd

I HEAR INGE'S SOFT SOBS as I watch her shoulders
move slowly up and down, up and down. I don't
know what to do, but I know I must do something
to make her feel comfortable here in Neuendorf. I need
her to feel comfortable with me, always with me. So, I
stroke her brown hair a couple of times and then her
neck a couple of times, and I can feel she is settling
down. *Ja*, she is calming down with me and for me. This
is good. This is good.

I help her up, and we slowly walk back to the big building. We enter the dining hall and sit at a long wooden
table. Her friend, Hilda, is here. "Inge, what is troubling
you? Why are you crying so?" Hilda tenderly asks. "Let me
sit by you, I will help you." For a moment, Inge opens her

eyes and turns her head just a little. She touches the apple Hilda has brought. The resistant skin of the apple is warm. I hold my breath just a little; maybe the sweet full aroma of the apple is enough to make her take a bite. One bite, Inge, please. One bite, I whisper under my breath.

"Gerd, could you get me a little knife?"

"*Ja. Ja,* Inge, right away. Right away," I answer. I bring her the paring knife, and she cuts small slivers of the apple and pushes a piece through her slightly open lips. This is good.

One by one, the cool days and cold nights settle in like a knit blanket covering Neuendorf. I enjoy working in the fields and feeding the chickens. And Inge, my Inge, now smiles every day. She is deliberate when she says, "Gerd, see how I have learned to wash the floors and to mend the clothes and iron. I am happy here." She has a full smile and melodic laugh. "Gerd, do you remember the first night of that awful bombing raid? The night we all had to go down into the basement of the main building, and you and I sat next to one another on that narrow wood bench? I think of that night when I trembled so. I am glad we found each other again."

Frequently when there are too many of us and too little work on the farm, Inge and Hilda and a few other girls are driven outside the farm to the little industrial town four miles away. Inge is apprenticed to a tailor and learns to make uniforms for the German army. I believe she is quite good at this sewing. Often, I am able to go to Berlin on little trips to take papers and documents for Weber. Of course, all the time I must wear that yellow Jewish star — the five-pointed star marked with indelible black ink with the word the Nazis call us: *Jude.*

After one of these trips, I learn that Inge has devised a way for me to be Jewish and not to be Jewish. "Gerd, I have something to show you," Inge tells me one morning. "From that tailor I am learning how to sew even the tiniest stitches. Look, Gerd, I cut a piece of black felt in the exact shape of the gold star. I took the thinnest sewing needle and black thread, and I have sewn a felt backing onto the star."

Inge turns the gold star over, laughs her hearty laugh and says, "In the middle of the felt fabric, I cut the thinnest slit with my small embroidery scissors. I hid a tiny safety pin just so," Inge says, as she shows me with pride the new backing.

"Inge, Inge, now I am able to put that star on and am able to take off that star. I can feel free again. I cannot believe this. You are clever, Inge, so clever!"

Today, as I prepare to do my Berlin errands, I walk in the middle of the road of this tainted city, holding tight to my bicycle and wearing no yellow star. I have no yellow star on, I repeat to myself. All the time I do this, I silently laugh at the Nazis who pass close to me, almost touching my arm, and I know exactly what Inge has done. I know exactly what we have done.

I do not mind thinking this way, because I gaze upon the distressed-looking people who walk along beside me. I can remember not so long ago, when I was a child, living here with my parents and sisters, when we would walk together on this street dotted with *stubels*, places of prayer — where so many men pray for so many hours on so many days. I did not really know what they were praying for or praying to.

On many mornings, we children walked with our mother to the kosher butcher and baker. I often would see these men standing in their shops' doorways dressed in their wrinkled, putty-colored jackets covering their long-sleeve shirts and slouched trousers, tucked into knee-high, flat-heeled boots, one hand in the pocket of their work-stained aprons.

"Children, would you like a taste of my newly cooked chicken? Maybe you would like a little piece of fresh-baked *challah*?"

"*Ja. Ja,*" I would answer. "Momma, is it OK?"

It always was all right with my mother. Then, we walked farther to the Jewish bookstore. We would go not only on holidays, but whenever we saved enough money to buy just one more book. On these special days, we would run up the steps and bound into our apartment to tell our father about our new purchase. I especially loved to sit next to him on our living room sofa to hear him read and tell his stories.

Today as I pass by the brick apartment building and think of my family living there, I remember when I was six we went on a Passover trip to my grandparents' farm in Zgierz, near Lodz, a small town in Poland. My father's parents lived in a one-room house made of plaster and wood, nestled on a little piece of land they were too poor to buy. Often, my father would send them money.

This house with one room was large enough; in one corner was the kitchen, and in one corner was my grandfather's workshop. My grandfather was proud to be a shoemaker, especially during World War I. He didn't tell us then, but later I found out that he would make glorious leather boots for Polish gentiles; he never got paid. I also learned there was more anti-Semitism in Poland than in Germany.

Oh, yes, we children had fun. I can see us now running all day through the grass, catching and kicking a black rubber ball, tugging a rope, and pulling water from the well in their backyard. My grandparents had no lock on their entrance door. I still hear my father saying, "This little house only had a hook that hinged."

There were eight children in that little house between our cousins and us. We slept in one tremendous bed in the very big one room. I remember how my grandmother sweetly tucked us in each night. We would say our *Shema* — our prayers — and as my grandmother kissed each one of us goodnight, she held a little, pointed paper bag filled with sweetness and love. She would place a little piece of rock candy on each of our tongues. This was the greatest treat in my life.

It is getting a bit cooler now. The dried leaves are circling in the air before settling on the cold sidewalk. I continue on my appointed rounds delivering the papers as I should. I am not looking where I am walking and almost bump into an Orthodox Jew dressed in his long, black coat and round, black hat. He holds the hands of a handsome little boy on one side and a sweet little girl on the other. Next to them on either side, are an older girl dressed in her long-waist smock dress and what seems to be an older brother in his pale knickers and shirt. They walk briskly by me, and I see that this Jew, who is wearing his yellow star, slightly raises his dark eyes my way. Maybe he recognizes me. Maybe I am afraid that he could recognize me. But, he is as careful as I am.

As the evening sky begins its nightly rounds, I sit in this open-back truck taking us back to Neuendorf, and I ask myself why exactly am I here. Is Neuendorf really a good place for me? Where else would I go? What else would I do with my life? And, then there is Inge. I think of her as we drive on this bumpy road, as I do so many times during my daily chores. *Ja*, I am happy that I work in this place. This work farm, Neuendorf, helps supply food for the town; this Neuendorf gives me money for the work I do every day. Ha, I don't even see the money I get, yet I know it is used for my room and board. I know that my soap, clothes, and shoes are given to me by a Jewish organization outside of here. *Ja*, this is a good home.

FOUR

*The sin of silence in the face of oppression is the
lesson of Kristallnacht.*

—Gerd

T HIS TRAIN IS DOING ITS JOB, like I do my job; it
is taking me back to this Neuendorf. Yet, I am so
tired, so tired of pushing my bicycle over the pock-
marked Berlin streets. Pushing my bicycle in and out of side
streets and keeping my head down and my mind alert.

Berlin is trembling. I am trembling.

The dull click-clack of the train wheels lull me into another time in my life, when I was fifteen and Hitler came to
town. I can still see November 9, 1938. November 9. November 9. *Ach!* It is still a chain around my neck. My mouth
fills with bile each time I speak of that cold, gray, depress-
ing day, a day filled with such trauma and pain, such misery
and fear, not only for us, but also for the Jews in our Berlin
neighborhood.

My father called, "Gerd, Rosa, Eva, come here. I have the radio on, you must listen. This is what I am hearing: There is vengeance upon the Jews," he chokes on his own words, "because some young Jew by the name of Herschel Grynszpan has shot some young man, this Ernst Von Rath, a junior secretary at the German embassy in Paris." My father pauses, "Children, this man is dead. This government man is dead." My father's face turns a pale white, like the white of an aged egg; little rivulets of purple make a circular map on his round face.

This retched day turns into retched night. My parents shut the lights in our apartment; we five stand by the window, looking down into the street. No one can talk. The shops already are closed. I cannot see one familiar face. Nobody is walking. And then, and then I hear this sound, a sound unlike any other I have heard. The pavement seems to buckle under the rumbling wheels of truckloads full of brown-shirted German storm troopers.

"Papa, what is this? What is going on?" I plead for some kind of answer, as these men jump out of the trucks in the intersection right in front of our building. They carry unlit torches, canisters filled with gasoline, and large heavy axes. I can hear crashing glass from the shop windows. They break down the heavy, wooden front doors and ransack everything inside. They torch everything. Everything.

Our Berlin neighbors begin to pour into the street. Some stand and watch, not knowing what to do. I see others run into the shops, carrying out food, clothing, radios, whatever they could get their hands on. I look up at my father for guidance. He utters only one word, "looters," and looks away... Across the street we see the Nazis break into our neighbors' apartments. They toss small furniture out of windows, rip open bed pillows, and shake the feathers out into the street into that jeering mob. The sound of shattered and broken glass is everywhere.

Then, we hear sirens and see smoke billowing from the direction of our synagogue, obscuring the view. Our temple, *'Die Alte Schul,'* is Berlin's oldest temple, my father's temple. It is sacred, and it is burning.

The sound of shattered glass is so frightening that my father decides it is no longer safe to remain in our apartment building. We put on our heavy coats and hats and leave by a rear door that goes to a side street. We inch along the buildings and try not to be noticed by the gangs of Nazis roaming the streets. We do not get very far when we see the SS carry out two scrolls of our Holy Torah from that burning synagogue. They roll the parchment all over the street; they trample it with their heavy boots. They torch it. The Torah burns.

Nearby, I see a group of bewildered elderly chassidic Jews, with bloody faces and chunks of their beards pulled out. I see the police standing nearby and they do nothing. They do nothing. We walk some more and finally make it to the non-Jewish section of Berlin, to the dark house of a German acquaintance. This man tentatively opens his door and he ushers us inside. "Only for the night," he whispers. We are so grateful. I cannot believe what is happening this night. I cannot believe these people are helping us.

I am awakened the next morning from my fitful sleep to find myself still dressed in my heavy coat. My parents and my sisters are still asleep on the floor. I almost do not know where I am. But, then I remember. The crash of broken glass still rings in my ears. My nostrils fill with the smell of flames that consumed our places of worship, our homes, our city, and our lives.

Our lives change forever. The Germans commanded my father to come here from Poland in 1917. He was just seventeen. He was a brilliant tailor. I remember his words, "Gerd, what was I to do? The Russians were overtaking Poland."

Our last name, Bocian, means stork. So, my parents live in that strong apartment building built near a stork's nest. My father often said, "Children, if that stork could make his nest strong with all this flying glass, then the Bocian family will be so strong."

I stand up and push the window curtain to the side just a little and look out on the street. People are beginning to come out of their homes; they take brooms and mops and begin to gather all that glass.

Someone is pushing on my arm. I come back from my memory as the train comes to a stop. I stand on my tired legs, find my bicycle, and push it to the door. As I look out the window and wait for the door to open, all that glass is still crashing.

FIVE

*These are bands of steel. No gold is allowed to
Jews. The cuts are perfect.*

—Gerd

O N THIS SUMMER AFTERNOON when the air is
damp from so much rain and the moving clouds
form pictures of black birds in flight, hungry rats,
wrinkled old women, and wrinkled old men, I find myself
sitting in my room here in Neuendorf and remembering
yesterday's train ride. I think again of my life at home with
my parents and my sisters.

I know what I have to do. I will go to see Inge. So,
I go to her building and place my clenched fist neatly
against her wooden door. A couple of times, I rap. A
couple of times, I rap again. "Inge, Inge, it is me, Gerd.
It is me, Gerd. Can you come out with me now? I need
to talk to you."

"Gerd, I hear you. I will be out in a minute. Just give me

time to wash my face and put on a clean dress," she answers. Even with the door between us, I breathe her in.

I take her hand in mine, and we go for a silent walk through the cool woods. Our shoes are getting wet. Our socks are getting wet. It doesn't matter; we are together. The damp leaves are sticking to our shoes, and bits of brown twigs are clinging to my pant legs. It is raining harder. We run a little, then we run fast and faster yet. By the time the rain falls in heavy sticks, we are running, running to find shelter.

"Inge, look, I see a small building not far ahead; we can go inside and get dry," I tell her. "We can stay until this rain finishes its soaking." Inge is shivering and too wet to answer. Her grip tightens in my slippery hand.

Finally, the little rain-soaked wooden shed gives us good shelter. As we take off our wet clothes and socks, and I pick off the burrs and little bits of branches from my pants, Inge curls into my arms like a kitten. She looks at me with her saucer-like brown eyes and quietly asks, "Gerd, you are still so silent even in this noisy rain. You are miles away from me. What are you thinking about?"

"I am thinking about us, Inge, about you and me and our days together here on this farm. I am thinking of what is going on outside of these brick buildings, outside of our safely tended gardens, away from the dairy cows we tend and away from the warmth of our kitchen. Inge, I am afraid the world outside is not safe any longer. I have word that my parents and sisters already have gone underground. I do not know where they are or how they are. I hear the safety of just being Jewish is in jeopardy. They already are taking away anything precious to us. They are rounding us up like cattle and taking us somewhere unknown. To the east, I hear. To the east."

I pull her closer still.

As Inge inches her tender body close to mine, and the rain sings a song on the roof, I slip my hand into my pants pocket and bring out a special gift for her.

"What are you holding, Gerd? Is it something for me?"

"Yes, Inge, yes," I answer. "You and I have been together three years now. We have become very close, so close that I never want to leave you. If we survive all of this…"

I can't talk anymore. So, I open my hand and offer her the hand-cut stainless steel engagement bands.

"Oh, Gerd, what have you done? Where did you ever get these beautiful bands?"

"I traded some food, some clothing, and got them from this man from the town. This is all I can give you today, Inge. I will give you more another time. If we survive, then we will marry."

Inge looks up at me and nods her head. I take one band and place it on her delicate finger. Inge takes the other band and puts it on my finger. With our hands clasped together, we stay wrapped around each other. Only the rain on the roof can be heard.

I get up off the floor to stretch my arms over my head. I bend my body first to the left, then to the right. Gently I lift Inge and massage her back a little to warm her. Her dress is just a little damp; the water marks on my trousers look like ripples in a stream. I wiggle my cold toes and put on my socks and shoes. Inge follows my lead. I am able to see bits of blue sky peeking through the clouds through the small square window.

It is time for Inge and me to open our door.

SIX

The Germans have us fooled. People couldn't
believe it. Nobody wants to believe it.

—Gerd

I HAVE BEEN THROUGH a thousand days and a thousand nights here in Neuendorf. In just two months it will be three years this farm has been my home. Finally, the black-and-white winter is making way for spring. Inge has found girlfriends, and they stay together as though they feel a chill in the air left from the winter cold and need each other to keep warm. Each day as I tend to two thousand chickens in this oversized hatchery, I often see Inge with her friends, Hannelore and Marlit, chattering together. As they walk arm-in-arm to their morning work, their woolen winter sweaters are buttoned to their necks as the early sun threads its way to the ground.

It is the middle of April, and yet I again am thinking of Palestine, but the little bits of news I am able to gather sit like a bitter onion in my stomach. This news is not good. It keeps me awake at night. Should I tell Inge, I ask myself? *Ja*, probably, I already know that Inge is aware; her frightened brown eyes don't lie to me.

At night, my friends and I sit in small groups to talk about what has been taking place in Berlin and in Germany. I worry about my parents and my sisters. I pray they are safe. I am friendly with a gentile worker here. He is a bricklayer, and a communist. He has a radio. We listen to the news in German and in English from the BBC and hear about the concentration camps. We don't believe it. If we get caught listening to these foreign broadcasts, we could get the death penalty. We are pretty scared.

I think about a cool September afternoon in 1939 when I am sixteen, and my father and I are walking down a Berlin street minding our own business, and this Nazi jumps out of the shadows and says, "Show me your papers! Show me your papers!" He reads. He checks our papers. He grabs my father and spurts, "You, you are Polish. You are not a German Jew, you are a Polish Jew." I remember the gleam in his eyes, the smirk on his face as my father shudders when this Nazi pushes him and pulls us a few hundred meters to this Berlin collection center. My arm is bruised and sore as we are pummeled and forced inside. The Nazi shoves us into a semi-darkened room with hundreds of other Polish-Jewish men and boys. My father and I are separated. The men go one way, the boys go another. I work in the kitchen and scrub floors. I polish everything. They make us do it, herding and chasing us around. We stay here for a few weeks. No one knows where we are, or if we are alive or dead. My father is beaten badly.

This anti-Semitism is surrounding us like barbed wire. My parents have a house in the woods, in the countryside near Berlin. One day, my father walks into the woods and sees, without any warning, a sign: "Jews are not allowed to enter this forest." The Nazis are everywhere. My father comes home a few hours later with blood dripping from his nose and his eyes. His black-and-blue cheek looks like a purple-and-green plum. He sells his house cheap.

Today reminds me of that purple-and-green plum. This Neuendorf land is swollen with piles of dirt from the fields, and the wind is blowing the birds from their nests for no reason. I hear someone calling me, "Gerd, Gerd, where are you? Where are you Gerd?" It is Inge, running so fast I hardly have time to catch her. "Gerd, do you not see what is happening here? This is the day, Gerd. We are going to the east. We are going to Eastern Europe to the concentration camps." Inge is breathless and crying and covered with this loose dirt. "Everyone has to pack heavy socks and boots, and clothes that we can carry. We don't know any more about it, Gerd. This is terrible, just terrible," she whimpers, as she looks down at her new engagement band. I touch mine, too.

My boots are covered with this dirt. I dig my sole into the earth, because I do not know what else to do. A few days before, the Gestapo is making lists. They always are making lists of us Jews. Then, Weber comes to tell me my job is too important here. The chickens need me, he says. Six of us are exempt. Maybe, I think, but for how long?

I cannot stand it. I go to the Commissar, the man in charge. I kneel down on my knees, "Let me go. Let me go," I beg. Weber grabs me and says, "Don't you know where they are going? Stay here. Stay here."

The next day they begin to load people on the trucks. Inge and I walk together hand-in-hand, close, so close together, we are one. Weber stands there with one of the Gestapo. He waves us over and points to Inge and says, "This is the girl. This is why he wants to leave." This Gestapo says to Inge, "Can you disappear?"

It is April 20, 1943. Some of us already went to Russia, to a ghetto. Some of us are lucky and have gone home to our parents. This last group to go huddles together like a pack of frightened dogs running around in circles. They wait. They wait.

"Kommen Sie hier! Kommen Sie hier! Erhalten Sie in linie. Sie mussen nicht stoben. Wir warden lben an bord helfen." Come here! Come here! Get in line. You don't have to push, we will assist you aboard." The SS officer waves his black stick in the air, as he commands that pack to move. Black dirt turns the road inside out; so many are packed into so many open-top transports. These young men and women raise their arms over their heads like they are clutching the air for help. I am close enough to see about 150 frightened faces.

Then I see just one face; I see Inge's face... I see Inge's face! She looks at me, and I look at her as I watch the last truck creep out of sight. I see the last bit of black dirt spit back at me from under the wheels and from under the weight of so many people.

After the trucks pull away, the Commissar comes back to me and says, "Mr. Bocian, were you satisfied with the way I sent your friends off?"

"Herr Commissar, I believe I can thank you for your humanity to my friends," I answer.

"Mr. Bocian, do you know what I've seen with my eyes? I watch as my wife and my son are sent away, too."

I cannot do anything but stay here on the farm. Truckloads of Ukrainian workers will help us now. My heart is not in this work anymore. Inge is gone. I do not know where those truckloads of people are really going; I only know they are going east. We stay together, the six of us young men. Somehow, we know we will survive.

We stay in Neuendorf for six months more. One bitter-cold October morning, we are ushered out of our beds, told to dress in warm clothing, put on our thick socks and work boots. There is no warning, just the piercing shrill of silver whistles and black-gloved SS guards pointing us toward the parked trucks. We put more pants, hats, sweaters, shirts, and our personal belongings into a woolen rucksack. We have no choice but to leave. You couldn't fool the Germans. The Ukrainians take our place.

We ride over the trodden fields for forty kilometers until we are in a place called Balendorf, a small forced labor camp in the surrounding forest. About twenty more people come here to work. This place, this Balendorf, is nothing nice. We live in a small run-down farmhouse and sleep crammed together in bunk beds and make our meals in a small, dirty kitchen. We can see we are on the grounds of a larger farm in a restricted location. The man in charge, a German forester, is very fair to us, but we cut trees for fourteen hours a day and must meet unreasonable quotas. My hands are blood red; my back is bent like a pretzel. I cannot see through the dense, overgrown forest. All the time I am exhausted. All the time I think of Inge. We don't know about Chanukah or Passover or any Jewish holiday. We don't feel anything.

We get bread and thick coffee for breakfast, watered-down soup for lunch, boiled potatoes for supper. I am hungry most of the time. Sometimes, I am able to pick carrots from the field or pull an apple from a tree. If I fell the trees and make the quota, I get Sunday off. I wash myself and my clothes once a week. I shave my beard once a week.

I am not really so unhappy. Yet, I can see the sky speckled with bombs as the earth shakes around me. I see the explosions. I am numb.

And then one day, I come back from work and something so amazing, so unusual happens to me. I cannot believe it. I cannot believe it. I am handed a dirty, worn letter, addressed to me: Gerhard Israel Bocian. It is postmarked from Auschwitz. No one gets mail here. Certainly, no one gets mail from Auschwitz. A second stamp, Frankfort Order, *Yudenstaten* (Jewish Department), shows me it was forwarded from Neuendorf.

Inge has written me a letter.

All I can think is she did not know I was no longer in Neuendorf when she sent it to the post office there. Probably some civilian forwarded it to me, because the Gestapo didn't see the Auschwitz postmark. *Ach*, Auschwitz.

I hurry to the outhouse so that no one sees me go in. I sit down. I must open this letter carefully — no one can see me do this. My hands shake. I can barely see through my eyes, but, *ja*, I must open it now.

SEVEN

I am No. 41910. I have no name.

—Inge

Sehr geehrter Gerd,
    Du fehlst mir Gerd, du fehlst mir. Oh, how I miss you, Gerd. We have been apart too long.
    I watched you watching me as I climbed into the truck. My eyes filled with tears, more tears than I even knew I had in my eyes. Gerd, I didn't want to leave you, I never want to leave you, Gerd. You are better off. Stay in Neuendorf.
    They pushed me into this transport filled with too many of us. There was no room to move or to even breathe. We were stuck together like hogs in a pen, like your chickens in that foul-smelling coop. We drove in this truck to the rail-road station. We were loaded on trains, in a baggage car. We stood so close together, so close, Gerd, so close, and we were packed like sardines. I couldn't tell where we were being

taken, but when the train finally stopped and we jumped off, I saw that the SS had ferocious dogs straining on their leads. Some of these dogs were let loose and they jumped on us. Between the barking and the whistles blowing, I could have gone deaf. Gerd, it was just awful.

When I looked around, I could see a dark, gray building. I thought maybe it was a factory. The SS pushed us inside and I could see better. I could see it was a school. Gerd, it was your Berlin Jewish High School! Gerd, the same high school founded by Moses Mendelssohn — the same philosopher you told me about so many times. Now I feel that you are with me.

I lay on the cold concrete floor next to another person. I kept my belongings close to me. I held them tight, even when I tried to sleep. I knew I couldn't leave anything far from me. Everything was stolen by someone to give to another for something more useful. Gerd, I couldn't do this.

I must take a break. I cannot read Inge's words much longer. My hands are shaking, and my legs are numb from sitting on this hard latrine. My watering eyes blur her words and make it even more difficult. So, I stand up, holding these pages tight and walk around in what little space there is. After a while I know I must continue reading. So, again I sit and read:

We stayed there four nights. We knew we would be sent away. We were given a bit of stale food sometimes, or a little drink of tepid water. Once a day we went outside for just one hour to get some air. We were taken to the back of the building to some kind of sports area. Sometimes we walked in the gymnasium. Outside was better. The SS made us march to music. Always marching, always music. Boys and girls marched together. We

*all wore boots on our feet, the same boots we wear for
work in Neuendorf. The SS tell us to sing. We sing songs
we know, songs from the Zionist Youth movement. We
sing loud for the SS:*

> *"We are fighting for freedom, equality and right
> We are fighting for Jewish honor
> We are demanding a new generation of Jews
> We are fighting for Jewish honor."*

*On the fifth day, we are herded into more cattle cars.
Marlit is with me this time. We found each other one of the
days we were marching and singing. Oh, Gerd, how good
it was to be with Marlit again.*

*We have to go. We have no idea where we are going.
My car is stuffed with too many boys and girls. We have no
water. We have no food. We wet ourselves. The car smells.
I wouldn't throw up; everyone around me is throwing up
and gasping for air, but there is no air. There are small
windows with metal bars at the top of this car. Sometimes
a big boy would hoist a smaller boy on his shoulders so he
could look out. What could he see? I don't know. Maybe
he saw the tops of trees. Maybe he saw a bit of gray sky. I
don't know.*

*Finally, we stopped. The heavy wooden doors are pushed
open. I see the SS and the dogs. I am so scared. They yelled,
"Out — out — out." I had to leave everything on the train.
We have to march. I stand with five friends. "Out — out
— out," they yelled again. The young ones marched to the
left, the older ones to the right.*

*Then I saw something that makes me shudder. There are
all these men and women, skinny-as-a-rail, bald people
in striped clothes running alongside of us from behind a
wire fence. Their big, dark blank eyes stare back at us. They*

keep yelling, "To work you are free. To work you are free." I
didn't yet know what they meant.

They march us to the side of a big hole in the ground.
"Take off your clothes," they yell, "take off all of your clothes."
I did as I was told. Then we march to a long, gray build-
ing. We stand there naked and shaking. Somebody pulls
me backward and starts shaving the hair on my head. He
shaved it all off, Gerd. Then he shaves the hair from all over
my body... from all over my body. My girlfriend calls to
me, "Inge, where are you?"

"I'm right here. I am right next to you," I answer. We
look like monkeys.

"Inge, we will get over this, I know we will. You will
see, one day far away from now, we will meet in New
York City."

Then they tattooed us... I am now No. 41910. I have
no name.

We had to go to a big washroom. We took cold showers
where there were no towels to dry ourselves. They shoved
one of those striped dirty uniforms at me. It is too big. I
wear it every day. They don't give us a clean one.

They tell us nothing. Nothing. They don't talk, they only
give commands. We have to run, not walk, everywhere.
Their whips and whistles and dogs are always close.

They separated us into two lines. One line went right to
the gas chamber. If they didn't like your face, you went to
the gas chamber.

I am put in one of the barracks with ten other girls. We
could sit on wood boards, maybe the size of a small couch. I
have no blanket, no sheet, and no pillow. I eat rancid soup
out of a filthy enamel bowl. In the morning, I go to work.
I hope my little bowl will be here when I come back in the
evening. Sometimes it is stolen. Maybe I am lucky to get
another one.

I go to the toilet in another big house. There is a big hole in the ground, like a big canal. I have to stand up; everything plunges in there. When I go to wash, there is only a little water dripping from the faucet. I have no toothbrush, no towel, just the cold water to wash my face.

I have to line up outside to get a meal. I eat on the board that is my bed in the barracks. Sometimes I have a 3-inch piece of bread. Sometimes I get a 3-inch piece of rye bread with a little watered-down soup, which could have little pieces of potato, sometimes some peas. You could find anything in that soup.

I am always hungry, Gerd. I am so hungry.

One day, the commander brought our belongings into the camp. Some other Jew clothes, maybe even some of the ones we saw running by the fence, the ones who have been here too long, who already know what they are doing, already sorted through the clothes. Some things were already thrown out; some things the SS kept for themselves. They took my shoes. I am wearing someone else's shoes now—they don't even match. One shoe is too tight. The SS took food we carried with us. From this they made our soup. I never saw my things again. If I was lucky, I could work under this commander, and could swipe some clothes once in a while. I would put on these clothes underneath, maybe I could be a little warmer.

Once, I worked outside the barracks with some civilians. Once, I got some sugar. I put it in my panties.

I met this woman, Margot Wicken, who likes me. I found out she is from my hometown—maybe she is my friend. She lives in the town of Auschwitz. She is the woman who gave me these pieces of paper and this pen. When nobody looked, I wrote this letter to you. She mailed it for me. Gerd, she says she can help me get more food. Can you send me something, Gerd? Can you send

food stamps and some money to this woman? I know she
will help.

I struggle to keep reading Inge's letter. I must finish it,
I know. I will memorize it. I will memorize the name and
address of Margot Wicken. Now I have to tear up this letter and put it in the latrine. I run to my friends, and I'm
probably stupid to tell them about this. They warn me:
"This is a trick, Gerd, the letter has been opened. Inge has
already been hanged." I cannot believe this. I do not want
to believe it. Not my Inge. No.

I wore a green, woolen, working jacket in Neuendorf. In
a corner of this jacket hem, my mother carefully had sewed
diamonds. I could use these secret gems for my welfare if
ever I needed to. I also had 5,000 German marks and trav-
elers ration cards. Food already is rationed in Germany. My
parents knew what they were doing. I've kept these whole
sheets of stamps folded in the bottom of my coat pocket.
Now, as I read Inge's letter, I know what I must do. So, I
go to this man, Garth Beck. He is a German worker, who
helps in the camp. I give him this envelope addressed to
Margot Wicken.

It all went too fast. I probably jeopardized our whole
group, as well as myself.

Eight

*In those crazy times of World War I, the Weimar
Republic and particularly during the time of the
Third Reich, anything was possible. no matter
how incredible it sounds.*

—Gerd

I AM EXHAUSTED. I am physically and mentally exhausted. I have read Inge's letter over and over again, until
it becomes part of my mind and my soul. I could recite
every line, word for word and not miss one sentence, one
breath of her being. Could it be that my friends are cor-
rect? Could it be that Inge already is dead? No, I do not
let myself believe that. I think of this letter that the Nazis
allowed through their mail system. This time, the clever
Nazis were not so clever.

I decide I must keep to my forest work, cut these trees,
and make my quota. If I do a good job, I could be rewarded.
And, if they make me march my way out of here, then I

will march. I will go wherever they want me to go. I have no choice.

This thought of marching brings back an important time in my life, a time after Kristallnacht when I was sixteen with my whole family in our Berlin apartment. The apartment has six large rooms, including two for my father's tailoring shop. In the apartment on the right side of us lives a middle-aged, black-hair, heavy black bearded chassidic rabbi, whom we know as the Warschauer Rav (The Warsaw Rabbi), who, in fact, did come from Warsaw. My father also was born in Poland, so he felt an affinity to this rabbi, whose given name was Kupfersztoch. He was the most well-known and highly respected Jewish personality in our *Scheunenviertel*. I was proud that he lived directly next door.

A few days after Kristallnacht, I ask my father if I could meet this rabbi.

"Papa, I think I saw this Rav coming out of his apartment when everyone was sweeping the broken glass. Do you think I could meet him? I am old enough," I remind him.

"We possibly could do that, my son," my father answers.

And so, we go next door to this rabbi's apartment and announce ourselves. It isn't a moment later that the heavy wooden door opens, and there is the Warsaw Rav.

"Hello, Rabbi," my father says. "I hope you remember me, I am your next-door neighbor. This is my son, Gerd, who has asked to meet you especially today. He tells me he saw you helping to sweep the glass. He thinks he even saw you walking down the street early this morning. Would it be possible for us to come in?" This gracious rabbi, this special man, is happy to have the company.

"And what can I do for you, my boy?" he asks.

"I have heard about you and how you saved your people. I wonder if you could tell me about it?" I ask him.

The rabbi ushers us in and offers us his comfortable sofa. He settles himself in his worn, comfortable, brown-tweed upholstered easy chair and begins. "In the days prior to World War I, I had a *shul* with about eighty to one hundred chassidic family followers. At that time, Warsaw belonged to Russia. The Russian army conscripted Orthodox Jewish young men into their military service. They were not allowed to practice their religious beliefs or eat kosher food. For those reasons, many of these draftees deserted from the Russian army. Among them were three of my brightest students.

"Just before sundown one night, three bodies could be seen swaying from three luminous, old oak trees, a hangman's noose tied around each neck. Dark, blank eyes stared into nothing."

The Rav breathes in so deeply that his whole body shakes like an earthquake stumbling through his soul. His eyes cloud over, his breath becomes shallow, and he says, "I swore at the foot of the gallows that I would avenge their deaths, and I would personally take revenge against the Russians."

The rabbi continues: "On August 1, 1914, World War I broke out when two Russian armies commanded by General Samsonov and General Paul von Rennenkampf invaded East Prussia. They fortified their positions near the so-called impenetrable Masurian swampy lake area."

He pauses a minute before he says, "Ah, my boy, nothing is foolproof. Nothing is foolproof." The Rav looks at me so intently that I rise up off the sofa and lean in a little closer. I don't want to miss anything.

"It happens, my boy, that the German General Hindenburg and General Ludendorff, in the Battle of Tannenberg, decisively defeat the Russians. This unlikely outcome happens because General Ludendorff receives the secret

Russian defense plans furnished to him by my very own espionage tactics." The Rav sits bolt upright in his chair; a furrow crosses his brow; his pitch is a notch higher. He speaks at the top of his voice. "Gerd, this victory, this surprising military victory led to the eventual surrender by the Russian Empire. Sometime later was the signing of a separate armistice." The Rav pauses a little and takes another wheeze-like breath. He drinks a little more water and settles once again in his chair.

"Now, young man, now this part of the story is unbelievable, unthinkable. It is practically unheard of, but it is all true." The Rav's words come quickly now; little bits of saliva sail from his mouth. His expression rapidly changes; his face turns beet red, and the words pour forth. "To express his gratitude personally toward me, Germany's Kaiser Wilhelm II arranges for me and my disciples to be brought to and to settle here in Berlin. They came by the hundreds to live in this *Scheunenviertel*. Even more astonishing and rare, the Kaiser grants me a *Reochspension*, a lifelong pension payable by the state."

The rabbi smiles. No, in fact, he breaks out into a hearty belly laugh which shakes the floor lamp beside him like heavy swaying branches from the oak tree outside our apartment.

"There is more to this story," he says. Without pretense, he adds:

"I became known as a special man. I have been given respect and honor always, even later by Germany's new president, Paul von Hindenburg. Every year, the people of Berlin can see me, with my long black beard, and my long black caftan, and my little rounded black hat, leaning on my cane as I proudly walk to the Presidential Palace. I go directly through the honor guard of the *Reichswehr*, the Regulars — not the SS — who raise their arms in deference to me, so I could always convey my own birthday wishes to President Hindenburg.

"I am proud to do this. I am proud that I came back to my *shul* with the address of Muenz Strasse 25. I am comfortable here. I preside at daily services and all the Jewish holidays."

Then, the rabbi slowly sits back and looks up at the ceiling, before he continues to speak: "Gerd, in 1933, when you were just ten years old, this man Hindenburg appoints Hitler the Chancellor of the Third Reich! One year later, Gerd, when the Nazis are in complete power, Hindenburg dies! But, Gerd, I am designated as a *Schutz jude*, a protected Jew. He has given me a state pension for the rest of my life."

Once more, the Rav settles himself and slides back against the soft chair cushion, ready to begin again. "You know how comfortable I was here; I held daily services and enjoyed presiding over all the holidays. Then something happened. In October 1938, during the *Polen Aktion* — the Poland Action — so many of my followers and maybe 15,000 former Jewish residents of Poland were deported. They were sent back to Poland. Two weeks later, just after *Kristallnacht* — the night of broken glass — thousands of these Berlin Jews and some of my followers were arrested. They were sent to the concentration camp, Sachsenhausen."

The Rav looks troubled. He rubs his reddened, runny eyes with his wrinkled handkerchief. He squirms in his chair. He scratches his forearm so much that blotches of darkened blood dampen his coat. But, he wants to continue. "You know how during the *Kristallnacht* all the Jewish businesses and homes on Muenz Strasse were vandalized. They were ruined. They were rubble. Gerd, all through this terrible night, this very terrible black night, posted in front of this building, this Muenz Strasse 14+16, where you and I live, were uniformed policemen. Even the Nazi SA — the storm troopers — were denied access."

The rabbi struggles to go on. He weeps openly, and yet he weeps with joy. He is like a stuffed rag doll trying to hold his place on the sofa. The Rav continues. "It seems like it was only yesterday morning when I decide to leave my apartment and travel to the outskirts of Berlin, to Oranjenburg, to the concentration camp, Sachenhausen. I demand an audience with the commander. After a long wait, the door opens, and I yell forcefully, "I demand the release of my people. I demand the release of my people."

"Gerd, I could almost hear the screaming and the yelling and the phones ringing and ringing," the rabbi says.

"And then as the sun is setting in the German sky, as the phones are put to rest, and the commander could do nothing else, the lines begin to form and the dust blows as I take my freed followers, and we all march out of Sachsenhausen. We all march out of Sachsenhausen."

This event is with me still. I remember the rabbi's words and his determination to free his people like it was yesterday. Here I am, in his dense, dark forest. Night is closing in, and that memory is so close. That old man will be my salvation. He will be Inge's salvation.

NINE

This is not a normal place. These are not ordinary times. We are being kept alive. But for what reason?

—Gerd

I REMEMBER SPENDING one more restless night here in Balendorf. The rough, splintery wooden board on my so-called bed bends and creaks with my body, as I move my sore arms and legs around in a circle, trying to find a place for myself. I cannot easily turn over, as the rotted board is so narrow, and the man next to me rolls almost on top of me all night. *Ja*, it is ok, I tell myself. *Ja*, I am still all right.

I spend the day in the damp cold woods, picking potatoes and carrots with the other men. All day I bend and pick, bend and pick. "Gerd, why do you bend over so low? Why don't you do as I do, and bend just a little and let your weary arms have a little rest?" I look up to see who is whispering to me. He shouldn't speak to me like this, we could get in trouble. I do not have an answer for him, only that I found a rhythm in my picking, and it works. The guards like it, they never bother me. I am not beaten with a stick about my head. I am not prodded with a sharp pole to my stomach and back, like some of the men. I do my job. I am a proud man always.

This isn't bad, this Balendorf. This isn't so bad. I lie here some more. I just lie quiet and think. Then, I think some more. At once the door opens, and this huge shadow of bulk obscures any bit of moonlight that tries to come through.

"*Guten abend*," he says with a drawn-out smirk. "*Such anziehen; aufstehen; gehen.*" he commands. We are to get up, get dressed, and we will walk a very long way. Again this walking. I pack my rucksack with my old, rotted clothing, my worn-out woolen socks and gloves without fingers, my tin plate, and tin mug.

We follow each other out the door, two together. Nobody says a word. The ground is still damp, and standing water seeps into my worn, leather boots and into my toes protruding from the holes in my socks. It doesn't matter. I walk in the footsteps of others.

But, I turn my head and look back to see this Balendorf, this home of my home, forty kilometers from Berlin. It isn't so bad here. We Jews have it better than the prisoners. We are the privileged Jews with preferred treatment. Our little group from Neuendorf is lucky to come here together. We always have each other. Not like the Russians or the Poles or the French prisoners who live in barracks and wear their army uniforms, we are separated in little buildings on the property. It isn't so bad. *Ja*, it isn't so bad.

The night wind whistles through threadbare trees, whose spindly branches sneer at me, beckon me to turn around and go back. Go back to what? Maybe ahead is better.

Ahead is a train station. I do not know where I am or how far I have walked to get here, but this is my new means of transport. The SS aren't so nice anymore. They herd us into people-packed cattle cars; so many people, so few cars. I cannot breathe, and there is no light. I don't know how long we travel, because time stands still for me. We whisper together, my little group and I. We are lucky we are still together. Wherever we are going, we will go there in our group. This is good. This is good.

The train begins to move. I am able to see a little stream of light creeping through a crack on the side of our compartment. I can almost see our faces and the faces of some of the Russian prisoners-of-war I have seen before. Then, I hear a voice I have heard before. This hoarse, cracking voice whispers, "Gerd, where are we going? Gerd, how can we survive in here in this heat? Gerd, help me. Help me." I know how he feels, because that is how I feel, like I am cracking, too. I take out my soiled, torn little piece of cloth, something I think of as my handkerchief, and wipe my brow. He cannot see me do this. I know he might see the shadow of my arm reach up to my forehead. *Ach*, we have something else in common.

The heat only bothers me for a little while. We stop almost as suddenly as we began. The heavy wooden door slides open, and I have to shade my eyes from the sun's brilliant glare. For a moment, I stop and look around. I know this place. I see my friend, Mordechai. "Look, my friend, look where we are, again we are in Berlin. They have taken us back to Berlin." I cannot believe it.

"I don't trust them, Gerd. This trip is too simple," Mordechai says. "They are going to do more with us, I can feel it. I just don't know how long they will keep us here. Yes, I am worried for you, for me, for us all."

So, my friend Mordechai is right. We are put in this city

block-long collection center. This huge stone building once was Berlin's police headquarters. It is next to Berlin's Jewish Hospital on Iranische Strasse. We are kept in groups of six or eight men. We sleep on mattresses on the floor. We are watched by a Jew named Blond, the guard who works for the Gestapo. Some Jews do this, to save their own lives.

We stay in this collection station for four or five days. We huddle together. They give us little watered-down food and even less watered-down coffee. Early one windy morning, we are once again ushered out of this filthy building. Again we walk to the train station. We are getting used to this.

With a loud hiss and an even louder crunching sound, the corroded train wheels screech to an abrupt halt along some forbidden railroad tracks. We are at a very dark, very secluded, very weary, train station. The heavy wooden doors are pulled apart by the SS, who have no patience for us now. Their slippery, wet, dirty, gray, attack dogs bark for their lives, as we push ourselves out of the train and onto a platform in a world we have yet to know. I see a worn wooden sign. It tells me we are in Bobusovice, a place I do not know, yet. We keep our rucksacks tight to our bodies and push-walk our way on damp gravel ground, following the man in front who leads the way for the man in back.

"Gerd, is that you?" I hear someone ask. "Gerd, where are we? Where are they taking us?" That voice again, the voice in the dark is calling out to me.

"I do not know," I whisper back. "Do not ask me any-more. We will both get beaten."

It seems that we are walking at least two kilometers when I see some lights ahead. I can only guess how long and how far we have walked, but my wet feet tell me I will not be able to go much farther.

There is a moat built around the place. I can see it through the trees. A moat, why do they need a moat? This moat is dry. I do not see any water here. I hear men talking in a Czechoslovakian dialect. I see they are wearing guard uniforms, and they are walking around everywhere. I see a sign: *Litomerice*. Then I see the word *Prague*. I don't see any SS. They move us to a *Schleuse*, a check point, where we turn over our possessions. I am humiliated that I must undress here. What are they looking for? I do not have jewelry, cigarettes, or money. I only have my rucksack, and now they have that, too. For this, I hang my head. I am ashamed for something I know nothing about.

I am told to go to this "house." I can see little houses everywhere. I see little dirty houses lined up along dirty walkways. I see dirty people sticking their heads out half-opened, dirty windows. We stare at one another. There, just ahead, on a wooden sign I see:

Ghetto Theresienstadt

But I don't see. What could I know more than what I hear whispered in our little group? This place, this Theresienstadt, this is my new home. Our group stays together, and this is good. They put us in these small houses; we cannot be comfortable here. The long, dank room is filled from floor to ceiling with triple-tiered beds. I find a bottom bed but could hardly move in what seems like a space no bigger than a baby's blanket, covered with rats, lice, flies and fleas. The humming noise coming from these vermin never stops. I try to cover my ears and my eyes, but they get into every hole. I want to jump away. There is no place to jump.

I could get away from it only once in a while, when I close my eyes and again see my childhood in Berlin as a schoolboy, perhaps nine or ten years of age. I would spend my vacation time on a nearby farm. There, I learned how to milk cows and to work with horses. The chicken incubation coop helped me when I was in Neuendorf. I always had people around me who I could depend on. From this, I could get certain privileges. *Ja*, maybe this would work here, too.

Now, I know a little more about this Theresienstadt, this ghetto-like town. Our group quickly learns to stay together. *Ja*, I am depressed some of the time, but not because I am so undernourished, I found a way to get around that. I am friends with this nice girl, Sarah, who sometimes gives me extra food. I never ask how she gets it. I just take it. We do that in our group — anybody helps anybody in the group. No one takes advantage of anyone in the group. Outside the group, maybe someone would take a chance, go on their own to save them. Someone would help himself to something that did not belong to him. I do not look right and left anymore, I stay within my group.

I know this one man, Havo Hansworth. He is motivated and a bit older than me. He is like a father to us all. Once, someone in our group took the wrong chance and tried to get away from here—sometimes someone who speaks Czech could try to get out of the ghetto—but mostly he would not make it, and Havo suffered because we lost so many people. He couldn't take it. He took me aside one day and said, "Gerd, I cannot watch what is happening here. I try to talk with other people, and when I do, my red-rimmed eyes tear even more. This is so hard for me. This is too hard."

Havo just gave up. He gave up and died.

Just like that. He died. I already have made up my mind that I would never let myself drop that low. I think daily of the people I love: my father, my mother, my sisters. I pray they are all right. Often, I remember that old broken down rabbi, the one who is called, The Warsaw Rav. I remember his courage, his will to live, and his will to travel far to save his people. I like to think if I keep his courage in my mind always, I can be like him. I can live. And, maybe I can save some people, too.

But it is Inge who I think of the most. My heart is with her, wherever she is, whatever she is doing. Day in and day out, it is Inge, Inge, Inge. The Nazis play this German song, they tell us the name, *Lili Marlene*. It is played day and night, night and day. The songstress has a beautiful voice. Maybe she is telling us something. I think they play it on purpose. My head aches when I hear it, and I wonder, does Inge hear this, too?

I come back to myself, and I know there is more here than this man, Havo Hansworth. Each day, the sun comes up, I get up, and I know a little more about my new surroundings. I learn through the underground, that this ghetto-town has enough room to hold 7,000 people. The Nazis have squeezed 30,000 to 60,000 people into this space. This cannot be, I tell myself. We are walking over each other. Every day, the streets are overflowing with people walking here and going there; walking there and coming back here. I walk in the footsteps of people I don't know. We are all walking in one big circle.

Then, I see the transports. If I could count, I would say there are about 2,000 Jews packed in these trucks going east. They empty the nest as fast as the nest is filled. I learn how cunning these Nazis are, they are clever. We have this Council of Elders — they have put this man, Paul Eppstein, in charge of this chosen group of Jewish, high-ranking prisoners. They decide who goes on these transports. I learn quickly that my work in the kitchen, feeding the prisoners, and sometimes feeding the Nazis keeps me privileged. *Ja*, I am in a good spot. I am privileged.

I work in this kitchen sometimes more than twelve hours at a time. I can do extra work here sometimes. They pay me in ghetto money, which equals to 100 krona. It isn't much. I buy mustard with this money.

I learn these are not normal times. This is not a normal place. The Gestapo has guidelines for distributing food and medicine. A few times a week, I see the sick and elderly walk slowly from their very old, little houses and stand in a line, trying to stand up straight, as they hold out unwashed, shriveled hands for a bit of food and a bit of medicine. We are being kept alive, but for what reason?

TEN

Hunger is a breaking point. There is panic to survive.

—Gerd

THESE NAZIS ALWAYS have a reason. Now, they have chosen this man, Eppstein, to be the head of the *Judenrat*, the commission of Jewish Leaders, the ruling Jewish body forced to enforce the Nazi decisions, like choosing who should be taken away.

"By tomorrow morning at 6 AM, I have to put so many Jews on these transports," Eppstein tells us. "The Nazis make me do this horrible thing. In my heart, I don't want to put anyone on these trains. But I must; I don't have a choice or they will kill me, too. I must do this, even if I know these people will be executed. These trains take them to Auschwitz to be gassed. So, either way, there is no other way."

Eppstein lowers his head and squeezes his eyes shut, and he trembles. I can see on his face that he is not ready to make a decision. Yet, in a matter of minutes, the Gestapo is upon him with their heavy black clubs. I cringe as I watch them almost beat the life out of him. His whole body is bruised black and blue. Finally they leave. Eppstein struggles silently to his feet. "I will live. I will live," he utters in short, difficult breaths. "I must live."

This happens so many times. This is a crazy place in a crazy world, where everybody tries to stay alive.

So, we have to make these reports to the Gestapo. I help with this. I am lucky. I am part of the underground. We falsify these reports and make them in duplicate. One set goes to the Gestapo. One set goes to the administration. We are careful what we put down. We have no choice, because everything has to be documented.

Now, they start. I watch as the trains are filled, not only with us Jews, but also with the SS and their official papers. Names of the most prominent people are listed first. They are to be exterminated immediately. I stand, and I watch silently as a new *Judenrat* takes the place of the old one. There is no evidence left.

Now, a new administration is immediately formed. The Gestapo looks for prominent Jewish people, who could pick their administration — friends, or whatever — anyone who is capable to work. These new men form a clique. They know that not everyone needs to be here. They all know what the end would be. They already have enough; for years they deal with the Gestapo.

Not everyone is chosen to be in this tight group. They do what we never did in Neuendorf: They steal from each other. I see them take medicine, bread, and sometimes cheese whenever we are lucky enough to have it. I have to ladle more soup into their tin bowls. I scoop the thickest part from the bottom of the pot, even from the burnt bottom. *Ja*, maybe it could be a little bit tasty. They look closely to make sure I give them the thickest potatoes in the soup. They grab for another piece of stale bread. I think to myself, "This is sad, human nature is sad." I keep doing my work.

Fewer people are here now. So, I am one of these people who stand and watch and watch and wait. Early one morning while I am standing outside the kitchen door with a little group, I see the elderly and the sick, walking with a sturdy branch as a cane, or on the arm of one stronger, get in line as the Gestapo decides how much medicine to give. I turn my head and whisper almost to anyone who is near, "The Gestapo is smart. They are giving medicine to those who look healthier. They want to keep them alive. For some reason, they want to keep them alive." I shake my head in bemused wonder.

I find the answer the next morning. As I am working in my kitchen preparing this watery soup, I hear footsteps outside my door. I hear many kinds of footsteps, some heavy, some a little bit lighter. And, I see as I go outside, lines of young people and young children are being pushed along by the Gestapo. The little children grab onto a hand of an older one, even someone they don't know. Maybe they think someone who is older will lead them in the right direction.

I watch them go out of the village right to the train. I hear the Gestapo shout, "*Weitergehen, weitergehen!*"—Move on, move on. The children cry, "*Mutter, mutter!*"—as they wail for their mothers. I cannot bear this. I go back inside. Even here, I hear the heavy train doors slide shut. I see the dingy smoke reach to the sky. They move east.

So, our Theresienstadt has fewer people today. Not all of the children have left; not all of the young men have left. I am still here, and there are many older people still walking around. There is much talk about the visitors, who soon will be coming. I see workers everywhere. I see an

old, rotted building on the center street being turned into
a Jewish bank. I see curtains being put up in windows that
yesterday were covered with dirt. I see baskets of bread,
trays of cookies, jars of hard candy, boxes of chocolates, all
brought into a newly painted grocery shop.

"*Ach*, we never have food like this. *Ach*, we never have
food," I tell Jacob, who is helping me chop rotten potatoes
for today's soup. "Look at those curtains," he says, "who
do you think is coming? Maybe we get a new, better administration," he says with a sly smile on his face. "Nah,
never that," I say. "We would have heard about this when
we were in our little group last night. *Ja*, the streets are being cleaned. Look, Jacob, look, they even put little red and
pink flowers in front of the children's houses."

The children do not live with their mothers. They live
in little *kinderheim*, little children's houses, that are never clean. Today they have flowers. Sometimes the Jewish
women, who teach them, smuggle in food for them. I ache
when I see their little dirty hands reach up for a small piece
of bread or for some cooked potato.

Today the women tell them something different. "*Mein
kinder* — my children, I have come to tell you we are having visitors very soon. They are people from the Interna-
tional Red Cross, who will come to see you, to see all of
us. Our *Commandant*, Rahm, has brought in new food for
us. He will give you lots and lots of chocolate to eat," the
Jewish teacher, Marta, tells them. "When he comes to see
you, you must answer, '*Onkel* — Uncle Rahm, don't give us
so much chocolate every day.'"

The children look puzzled. They never have candy of any
kind, certainly not ever chocolate candy. I watch these sad-
looking little children every day. It is a pity to watch them.
Instead of growing up, they shrink.

This place has many important people, such as singers

who find the words to sing, musicians—who have come here carrying their instruments—and find music to play, and actors, and artists who find paper to paint. I see them carrying torn bed sheets to use as painting canvases. They secretly come to teach the children how to draw. One artist takes these children's drawings and hides them in a suitcase.

Sometimes, I watch the actors and the singers and wonderful musicians, who practice the Verdi Requiem. One day, the SS arrive for a cultural event, like this is something they do every day. It is our people who perform this for the Red Cross and for Rahm. But the prisoners know this whole thing is a sham. They must play along, or they will be punished. The underground tells me, when the Red Cross passes in front of them, they whisper, "This is fake."

ELEVEN

We go to the railroad station to help open the
cattle cars. The skeleton corpses fall out at our feet.
The lucky ones are alive.

—Gerd

IT IS ALL A FAKE. Everything; all of it is fake. The Red Cross visit was a fake. To me, I am living a nightmare. This Theresienstadt, this is nothing more than a rotted piece of vomit-colored soil. Since the Red Cross visitors have left, the Jewish Ghetto Police, those prisoners who save themselves by using their whips and clubs on us and take us to their jail, have taken over again. They have been chosen to keep internal order. They impress the Gestapo. They do not impress me.

Even this man Eppstein, this German Jew, they put in charge. He thought he is doing the right thing for us. Ha, what right thing? Bang! Bang! I hear another bullet and again the trumpeting triumph of another bullet. Eppstein is eliminated. Eppstein is shot. Ha, they have no more use for him.

My daily routine is once again my schedule of daylong cooking and scrubbing out oversize steel kettles. "Jacob, this work is killing me," I tell my kitchen friend. "Here, we stay on our feet all day long to cook more soup to feed these people." At least in here we can talk freely. "But, Gerd, this will come to something. This will come to something soon. I can feel it. I stand here and cook just like you, but just this process of cooking and scrubbing keeps me alive. My legs ache, my hands are the color of red clay, just like yours. But, something tells me this will all be over soon." I listen to Jacob's repeated response. I always listen, because he could be right. He could be right.

We thought the warm days of spring would bring renewed hope to us all. Nothing is ever as it should be in this place. Without notice, not long after the Red Cross leave, Eichmann comes back and orders Commandant Rahm to begin building gas chambers. These gas chambers would kill all of us left in this camp.

Jacob comes running and yelling, "Gerd, Gerd, I saw trucks coming into camp carrying the gas!" I turn around and see just what he is telling me. Then, I see one of our largest buildings will be used as a gas chamber. "This can't be happening to us," I say. "Not now. Not when I feel our days should be getting brighter, not darker."

More news comes from the underground. They tell us the Germans have learned the Russians are moving closer to Prague. The next morning, a resistance officer comes in and proposes to Rahm that he might be able to save his life at war's end if he spares the Jews. A Red Cross official comes back and negotiates with Rahm that he would personally take him out to Switzerland.

Could it be that Rahm would make such a deal? *Ja*, he

could probably do this against Eichmann's orders. Maybe this would keep him alive. Rahm is not stupid. He knows he could be tried as a war criminal if he follows through with these orders to gas thousands of inmates here. I learn more from the underground that Rahm procrastinates enough to let the Red Cross take him out during the night.

I live from day to day, not knowing what will come next. A new _Judenrat_ is put in place with a man by the name of Murmelstein, a well known rabbi from Vienna. These Nazis know how to find the most prominent Jews, and they put them here. But 'here' is no place for them, now. He tries to keep peace for almost five months, but in the beginning of May, the sky is darkened with many jet planes coming closer and closer. I look up and hear the loud whistle and even louder roar of Russian bombs attacking just outside our little ghetto.

"They have come. They have come to save us!" I shout to everyone in my group. Looking up at the sky, I raise my arms and shout, "Welcome! Welcome! Welcome!"

I hear the sound of heavy artillery for two weeks. This artillery comes closer and closer. I know it is only a matter of days now that we will be saved. For the first time, I talk to that God I almost didn't believe in any longer and utter, "_danke, danke, danke._" Now, I can finally thank him.

In the morning as I walk to the kitchen, something is different. I do not see the SS. The SS have disappeared. It isn't until the Russian tanks come in that I realize we are free. In these last days of the war, as Germany shrinks more and more, they take Jewish prisoners along whenever they retreat. Now all these people have been transported to Theresienstadt. Day and night I cook. Sometimes I work eighteen hours a day to make more food for all these people. I can eat as much as I want. I give them as much as they can chew. Their bone-thin bodies look like skeletons.

Their blue-striped shirts hang on their bodies like dirty rags. Their feet are scored with purple-colored dried blood. Some of them in cattle cars survived by drinking their own urine. They look more dead than alive.

I stay here to help the sick and the dying. I need to keep cooking, to help save as many as I can. I remember standing outside of this ghetto, on one of the nearby streets — I don't remember how I came here — and I see a large wooden wall built by the Nazis. I am with my group and we tear it down. More Russian tanks appear. They are loaded with cigarettes and cigars. They see us. We raise our arms up to them for help. They throw the cigars and cigarettes to us. I never see so many men falling to their knees as we pick up this forbidden treat.

I go to the railroad station again to open the doors of these worn-out cattle cars. I see a lot of tired people. I come upon a sad-looking, shriveled, filthy man. "Gerd," he calls out my name, "Gerd," he calls out again. I think maybe he knows me from Neuendorf.

He barely crawls over to me, as his feet scratch the ground and bleed. His tongue hangs out, and his bloodshot eyes bulge as he reaches up for my hand and says, "Gerd, I saw Inge in Auschwitz."

TWELVE

I don't want to think... I work right there... I
could smell it all night. The gas chamber.

—Inge

IS IT STILL POSSIBLE? Inge is alive? For all these
months, Inge has been in Auschwitz. I cannot believe it, but I want to believe it. Of course, of course,
she would take care of herself, she is smart. She let me
know that in her letter sent from Auschwitz—how
courageous that was—how perceptive of her to give it
to Margot Wicken and for that brave woman to take
the letter to a post office. *Ach*, they could have cut off
her hands.

I have to sit down, just like I sat down when I was
handed that four-page letter so long ago. I hear in my
mind this man's words over and over again. Inge is alive.
Inge is alive. I can picture her, my beautiful, dark-haired,
piercing big brown eyes Inge. Her smile and soft skin is

like an angel. Yet, I can picture her sitting there in that dark, damp, disgusting place, writing to me.

In Auschwitz, we have bunks with threadbare little blankets. It is a little cleaner here. I feel a little better. Sometimes, I can go and wash myself. I still don't feel like a girl, I am still a monkey. I wear my kerchief all the time. My hair is growing back a little each day.

Here, I live with different people, but they all look like me. Czechs, Slovaks, Poles, Dutch, Greek, and French and from Belgium. I know that certain groups are selected to come here. The non-Jewish political prisoners are identified by the green triangles sewn on their shirts. They don't go to selection, they only work in the kitchen. I don't see any Gypsies here. Gerd, I hear the girls whisper about having to be prostitutes for the SS. I am lucky no one has taken me to do this.

We are told to sew and wash for the SS. Some people I see from the munitions factory. I look around and see mostly Jews. I hide when I see the SS coming. I know they come to hit us. Gerd, they are always hitting the Jews! They take out their whips and swing 25 lashes on our behind... 25 times they hit us... for nothing, for no reason at all. They just hit us. One time, this girl was looking for her blanket. Someone stole her blanket. They hit her because she had no blanket.

One day, I see this Jewish girl trying to escape. Oh, Gerd, I am so scared for her; all the time I am trembling. So, she runs...and she gets caught...the SS strap her behind a wagon, her feet hang down on the ground. The heels of her feet drag on the rocky brown dirt road. I watch as she is pulled through the whole camp that way. I see the bloody stumps of her heels, and I see her feet where her toes should have been, and I watch her weave a path to nowhere. We Jews watch and we watch, and we watch her die. She dies. Gerd... she is no more!

Ach, what is this I am reliving in my mind? What is my Inge saying to me? Such sinful stories come from this soft girl. This girl, this is my Inge. My hands are shaking, just like I am still holding those papers. Drops of water cloud my eyes. Is it raining? Nah, this is not rain, it is my tears running down my face onto my own outstretched hands. My tears can make Inge's words disappear from my mind. This cannot happen.

How did I stand up? When did I stand up? I take a deep breath, let out a long sigh and sit down again. I close my eyes, and again the memory becomes clear.

Gerd, it is always so cold in the barracks. The cold air presses on my bladder all the time. It is always the cold air and the thin, tepid soup that give me a stomach ache. Once, in the middle of the night, I have to go to the toilet. I can't hold it in anymore. So, I go out the door, but I can't make it to the toilet. The SS sees me. I have to sit on my knees in that cold air, just in front of my barracks. I sit there and he tells me to stay like a dog. The SS walks back and forth, back and forth. First in front of me, then in back of me. He walks. I shiver. When I see he is gone, I go back into the barracks.

I am still frozen and shaking by morning. Then, it is time for work. I stumble my way to the munitions factory. I have to work. I have to tell you something, Gerd. I have to tell you they think I am working all the time just for them. I feel that I am lucky, Gerd. I am so lucky. The icy January winds blow all around us, and the earth is frozen under my feet. I am lucky to wear these heavy boots. I am lucky someone gave them to me. I never know who does these things, they just happen.

We girls work together with the men. I sneak my hand under the scarf tied on my head and put little bits of gunpowder under it. I smuggle it outside, where the men are waiting. When the Sonderkommando, those Jews who work in the crematoria, aren't looking, I pass this gunpowder to the men. Who knows how many times I do this. One morning in the middle of January, I hear the loudest bang, so loud the ground shakes. The gray sky is filled with black smoke. Whistles are blowing, and the dogs are barking. People run everywhere. They blew it up — Gerd, they blew up the crematoria!

They blew it up when no one was in there.

I can almost feel that this is the beginning of the end for us. I don't hear any more noise outside. I cannot believe it. The dogs are quiet, no whistles blow. I stop working just for a minute. The SS aren't screaming for us to line up outside. I take a chance and open the door a crack. It is so dark outside. The smoke takes the light away, and I cannot see anything. Then, the noise starts again. Only this time it is different. I can see dust blown up from the ground. I hear the sound of large transports rolling into camp. Gerd, I am still scared.

Now, the SS come at us and move us outside. We are all in a line, and we must walk and walk, all through the night. These heavy boots protect my freezing feet. The SS push us with their rifles. We hear the noise of planes flying overhead sometimes. We have to lie down and hide in the grass. The SS don't stay with us when this happens, so I say, "Wait, wait," but the rifles and the pushing don't allow waiting. We walk into the forest. We have to go, or they will shoot us. I can not run away. I have no food. I step over rotted wood from fallen trees. I push low-hanging branches, dense with brown and green leaves, off my face. I try to lick the little bits of water off the wet leaves that stick to my face. My dress is covered with twigs. I keep walking. I keep walking.

A lot of people die on this march. We eat the rotten potatoes we find on the ground. I am lucky, I eat these potatoes, and I don't feel so hungry for a while.

Inge's letter stops here. I must stop thinking about this. I want to know more, but I cannot think anymore. My head is on fire, like the burning landscape around Theresienstadt. There are too many people here trying to get out of the village. Too many people need to get away from here. I need to get away. I need to get back to my family in Berlin. I hope my parents and sisters have survived underground. They are cunning and smart like the Warsaw Rabbi, like Inge, like me.

First, it was Inge's letter that I remembered. Now, I see another clear vision. Again I see him. I see the Warsaw Rav walking through the woods and through the streets of Berlin, his body wracked with pain, his hand gripped tight around the handle of his crooked cane, walking, walking to get his imprisoned men out of that Sachsenhausen concentration camp. Thoughts of this Rav are giving me the courage to get home. I have thoughts of my Inge walking, walking just like the Rav, and like him, she, too, will have courage to find her way back to me. I know Inge will come back to me.

I have spent enough time here in this camp Theresienstadt. It is time for me to leave. Finally I feel free. *Ja*, I am so undernourished and weak, but I am young, and I can take care of myself. The Russian troops are giving us back our life. So, I carry my rucksack again with pride, and I walk out of Theresienstadt. Forever.

I am with my little group. Always I am with this group of men. We climb up on the back of a truck going to Dresden. What a comfort it is to know that I am going home. This truck takes us to a train station, where I see a locomotive, and I see a word printed on the side of a car: "Berlin."

I am told only two of us Jews can go, and only if we stoke the coal. I shoveled coal for days. How many days, I do not know.

Finally, the wheels slow down, the train is stopping. I

take my rucksack and jump off. My eyes slowly adjust, and I know I have made it back. I am home. But I don't recognize my Berlin. The tall buildings are now half buildings. What used to be is just piles of rubble. I kick my feet into this rubble. I feel like I am kicking life.

So many shops that used to be open to us do not have doors. I remember all the glass from *Kristallnacht*, but this is worse. I see so many people: soldiers coming back, skinny, stooped-over people in their dirty striped jackets and pants. They are walking these well-known streets, but now these are streets with no names. These people have faces with no names. They walk to apartment buildings with no walls, no people, no laughter. Nothing.

Except one. Our apartment building in the middle of this block called Muenz Strasse is surrounded by broken bricks, but it has doors, it has windows, it has people looking out at me as I look in at them. This building with the apartment of the Warsaw Rav, the apartment next to ours, is still standing. Our apartment building is still standing.

Ah, *ja*, I remember. This rabbi is special, he is a *Geschutz jude*, a man protected by the state. I rush up to the second floor and push open the door to my parents' apartment.

They are all here — they are alive: my mother, my father, my two sisters — they are alive! I cannot believe this — we grab each other, we kiss, we hug, we dance in a circle. We weep, we laugh, we weep some more.

"Gerd, oh, Gerd, you are home. You are alive," my father cries out, half crying and half choking as he takes me in his arms and cries some more. I am crying, too. He takes my face in his two hands and with half tears and half voice, he says, "Gerd, you are home safe. You are my safe son."

THIRTEEN

We were vermin, not human. The Germans tell
us over and over again.

—Gerd

JA, I AM HIS SON. I will always be my father's son and my mother's dear boy. I am brother to Rosa and Eva. Now, I know I will always be here for them. They have proved they will be here for me. I know our strong family name has kept us alive: Bocian.

"Papa, Papa, you are all here; you are all well, a little undernourished, but you are here. Your furniture is still here." I turn and point to the worn sofa, to the over-stuffed chairs, to the dining room table, the lamps... I cannot believe what I am seeing. "How could this happen?"

"I will tell you, my boy, I will tell you," my father says looking directly at my eyes. My eyes are filled with water, but I look directly back at him. "As difficult as it is for me to tell you, your mother and I were drafted into forced la-

bor in the Siemens plant. Here, we made ammunition for
the German army.

"In the spring of 1943, when we hoped you were still in
Neuendorf, many of the Jews, even those doing this forced
labor, were arrested and deported. In the middle of one
night, your mother, your sisters and I left our apartment.
We carried with us just our blankets. We wore layers of
our clothes, and we quietly crept along the shadows. Every time we heard an unusual noise, we stopped, we didn't
move, we didn't speak. Finally, we gently knocked on the
door of a gentile family that I know, and who had told me
they would help us, if it ever came to that."

I had heard stories like this from my little group in Neuendorf. So many families kept alive this way, but I couldn't
believe it of my own family. How lucky they were.

My father looked at me again. I knew he wanted to
say more.

"Gerd, my Gerd, for all these years we were kept alive.
Like we sewed the diamonds in the lining of your heavy
green jacket, I gave these people some of the hidden money and the diamonds in our coats. They kept us in their root
cellar along with the rats and vermin. But they were true
to us and every few days brought us a little food and water.
We could not have lived without their help."

My father relaxed a little. He went to the sink and
poured himself a glass of water. How thin and tired he
looks. How much strength he has to live. I am shocked
and relieved.

Coming back into our living room, he settles into his
favorite big chair and motions for me to pull over a chair
to be close to him. "Gerd, there is more," he tells me. "And,
Gerd, because of this man, this Warsaw Rav, our next-
door neighbor, the Nazis put Gestapo all over this building. Some of them lived in the rabbi's apartment. Some of

them lived in this apartment. There was a police guard all day and all night outside watching our apartment building. When the war ended, this Gestapo functionary also abandoned our apartment. When we could move back in, what do you think we saw? Gerd, we saw all this furniture. We found most of our possessions. So much was saved. So much was saved."

They are cunning, these Nazis. Look what they do to make life easy for themselves. How lucky we are they put one of their own into my parents' apartment. Look what this Warsaw Rabbi did and didn't know it.

For weeks, my mother arranges her furniture and puts out some saved family possessions. We are comfortable again. My home is my home again. But it is not really my home. With my eyes looking only at the floor, I say, "Mama, Papa, I have something to tell you. In Neuendorf, I watched helplessly as Inge was put on a transport to the east. I didn't know where she went until one day I received a forbidden letter from Auschwitz. This letter was written in small letters, on four sides of little pieces of paper. It was from Inge."

My father stumbles backward. My mother gasps and puts her hands over her mouth. "Is she alive, Gerd? Is Inge alive?" my mother questions. "A few months ago, a man told me he saw Inge in Auschwitz," I answer. "I don't know where she is or if she is still alive. Maybe she has gone home to Herne to find her brother. It could be she is hurt." My throat closes up.

As I run to our front door, I turn back just enough to tell them, "I am going to look for Inge. I am going to the Jewish Hospital."

FOURTEEN

We give thanks to God for what he does to us, for this nightmare may never be solved.
—Gerd

I AM A QUIET MAN, but I can hardly hold in my excitement, my sense of security to know I will find Inge. I run to the Jewish Hospital and cry out her name. I beg this person sitting at the desk to tell me if she is here and where I can find Inge. It is taking too long. This man looks and he looks, and he checks his papers one more time. I ask him to check again. Exhausted, he looks up at me and says, "*Nicht finden konnen, ihren Namen hier. Inge Franke ist nicht hier.* — I cannot find her name here. Inge Franke is not here." I repeat those words over again until the pain in my head is so bad, so bad. I must leave this hospital.

I walk out the doors to the street overflowing with refugees. So many people are walking around looking for so many other people walking around. My head pounds with rage and fear. The searing, burning pain won't go away. I see my friend, Amnon, and in a voice choked with tears, I say, "Come with me, come Amnon, we must go to the west. Maybe Inge has gone to Herne." My group, the men with me in Neuendorf, Behlendorf, and in Theresienstadt, have garnered a truck. I climb in this truck to drive to the River Elbe, the organized border between Russia and Germany.

I am riding for a little while, when I poke my head out the open window and see a dark-haired young woman pedaling her bicycle. So fast she is going. So fast she peddles. I watch her closely as she pedals toward me. I look closer as her dark hair blows in the wind. Her open jacket is flapping behind her, her feet pedal in ferocious circles — faster, faster — and faster she goes. I poke my head farther out the window. *Oy, oy,* "Stop this truck, Amnon! Stop this truck!" I see Rosa, my older sister Rosa, pedaling, pedaling, as she tries to catch up with our truck. She calls to me, "Gerd, Gerd stop this truck. Inge is alive. She's here. Inge is home."

The truck couldn't go back fast enough for me. I jump out the door as the truck slows down; I couldn't wait for it to stop.

I stand on the street, my knees are shaking. I look up to see Inge peering out the window of my parents' apartment. When she sees me, she runs out the front door, down the rickety steps, into my arms. *Ach,* she is so small, she is so skinny, but those brown eyes tell me it is really Inge. Her skin is worn and sticky from dirt. She is wearing at least four layers of clothes. A torn, dirty striped jacket is all I can see as she puts her arms around me. We stay this way for what seems to be forever. We cannot let go of each other. For such a long time, we cannot speak. We look at each other and do not let go. When we finally undo ourselves, Inge's torn jacket sleeve falls away from her body. On her arm, I see the tattooed number: 41910.

Ach, what she must have been through. How brave she must have been. We begin to take a little walk. It is so good to feel Inge again. Inge is home. Hand in hand we hold onto each other, just like we did that rainy day in Neuendorf when we took refuge in the wooden shed, and with those metal rings we pledged ourselves to each other.

With so much fear and anticipation, I must hear her story. Inge has found me. She has come back to our Berlin. "Inge, come, Inge, let us find shade under this tree. There are not so many people." I take her hands in both of my hands and look into those big brown eyes before I say, "Tell me where you have been all these months." Inge is half crying, half speaking, as she begins to talk to me. "_Gerd, komen ie, setzen sie sich hin. Ich muss Ihen sagen, was mir passiert ist_ — Gerd, come sit down, I am ready to tell you what happened to me."

Inge begins to slowly speak. "Gerd, we heard the planes and then the trucks. The Germans pushed us out of camp. We were made to walk so far through so many woods. We walked to this place called Ravensbruck, a special camp for women. We stayed there for two or three days—I don't remember exactly. They gave us some food. At night, we girls talked together about the noise I heard that last night in Auschwitz. It was the Soviet forces coming to liberate us. Now that I realize this, I think, why was I marching? The SS were clever; they took us away so they could get away."

I put my arm around her and softly say, "Inge, I have heard about this march. I could not believe what I heard. And now to know that you were part of this, _ach, ach..._" My head aches. My heart is pounding. Yet, she wants to say more.

"By morning I had to march again. This time, I went to a place called Molchau. It was a little camp with so many people already there. I stayed for one week, but I didn't have to work. They gave us food once a day. It was not much food, but it was better than that awful soup. We slept on the floor in this big room. I didn't have a blanket. I rested my head on my arms.

"I was relieved that the week went by quickly. After that, they took us by baggage cars to Stuttgart. All the while, I heard bombs going off. I saw flashing lights all around me. By daylight we walked to a field studded with tall bales of hay. One German said, 'Come with me.' Nobody went. I don't want to know what he wanted."

"You were always cautious, Inge. This is good. This is good." I put my arm around her tighter as the weather turned cooler. The German sky is always filled with gray shadows. We stand up and move to another place down the street. Here, we find a partially intact metal bench and make ourselves comfortable. I think to myself, oy, what she has gone through. I feel sick thinking about her in those woods.

Inge looks up at me as she says, "Gerd, maybe now there were thirty of us left from the camp. Five of us walked to a little town called Risa. We saw a soldier. Oh, my God, I thought I was back in the hands of the SS. He was not an SS, just a soldier there in this little town.

"The five of us went together to the mayor. We never said we are Jews, even though I wore this striped jacket over my clothes. He didn't say anything. He gave us a little food and a place to sleep. He put us in this little nursery building. All around were little cots. There was a toilet, lucky for us, because we had diarrhea. Gerd, I saw some blood, but I didn't tell anyone. I was scared. In the evening, we went for a walk. We came to this farmer and asked him for food. We took the food and put it in our pockets.

"We stayed in Risa for one week. The German SS left. One day, two Russian soldiers came into town. One said to me, 'Come and sit on my lap.' I tell him, 'No, no, I am

Americansky.' It just came to my head to say that. 'You are *Americansky?*' he asked. With all my strength, I told him, 'Yes.' I don't know how it happened, but it saved both of us. He didn't know English, either. Then, he showed us his watches and rings. He went out and brought us back food, and he left."

"Inge, do you want to go upstairs to my parents' apartment now?"

"No, Gerd, let me finish. I need to tell you all of this first, then we go to your family. But, there I don't want to talk about it again."

So, Inge continues. "Just my friend, Annie, and I wanted to go to Berlin. The other girls went to the west. I needed to find you, Gerd. We were in this place known as the State of Saxonia, it was one of the new little village areas the Russians put together. The weather was getting warmer, and I asked Annie, 'What is the date today?' I didn't know why, but I needed to know that. Annie answers, 'It is April 20th, Inge, it is April 20th.'

"We walked, and we walked to a railroad station and got on a train to Berlin. We didn't have a ticket. We just got on. They let us on, anyway. We asked people for food and money. You know, they gave it to us. We went on more trains. It took us a week to get here. Now, I know that I was really liberated.

"Now, I am here. I looked for your parents' apartment. All I saw were bombed-out buildings. 'That's where their house was before,' I say to Annie. Then this man in a white butcher coat came up to us. 'Who are you looking for?' he asked. 'The Bocians,' I tell him. 'You are the future daughter-in-law?' he asks me. 'Yes,' I tell him. He points to the other side of the street and says, 'That is the apartment building.'

"I looked through the keyhole and saw an old lady sitting in a chair. Just then, your sister came out the door. She looked at me. I looked at her. I didn't know what to do. I was trembling. She was trembling. We grabbed onto each other, and all we could do was cry. Tears ran down my cheeks. Her cheeks were wet, too. Our tears mixed together, just like we were already family. Then, she clutched my shoulders and looked at me so hard, like she was boring a hole in my head.

"'Gerd is back,' she said. 'He went looking for you. He thought you were hurt. Then, his friends got this truck to go to the border. Maybe they think you went to Herne to find your brother. Inge, wait here,' she tells me. She gets on her bicycle and goes to look for you."

Inge becomes very quiet when she finishes her story. I do not want to upset her any more by letting her know how upset yet how happy I am that she is home. I am numb. I have not felt this way since I watched her leave from Neuendorf on that open truck. But, she is here, and I am here, and we will be fine. We slowly walk to my parents' apartment.

FIFTEEN

*People should be really careful it shouldn't happen
again. If Israel goes down, all Jewish people will
go down.*

—*Gerd*

IT IS TWO WEEKS NOW that Inge and I are in my parents' apartment. She does not say much anymore. Inge has shared her nightmare with me, that is her privilege. We all walk around like ghosts, who choose to hover over corpses. Our words are whispers. We shake our heads back and forth, all the time back and forth, and we look upward. What are we looking for? Is someone up there who can offer us advice?

Our Berlin is still a mess. My father sometimes goes outside, perhaps to find a friend, or just to walk in this city he remembers. "How are you this morning, Mr. Bocian?" asks the butcher, who every day sweeps his shop and nails up wooden boards where windows and walls should have been. "I cannot offer you any meat today, Mr. Bocian, but I wish you a better day today than yesterday," he offers. "I am well, sir, I am well. Can you believe this? Can you believe my whole family is with me again?" My father continues on his walk.

It is time for Inge and me to venture out of doors. Her gray skin is beginning to show a bit of pink... I lift up her chin with my finger and almost see life in her brown eyes. "Come Inge," I say. "Come, together we will walk to the displaced person's center. Let us see who might be there." Inge puts on a sweater and walks timidly out our door.

So many people have congregated inside. So many refugees return to memories. So many memories here, and too much of their story is too familiar. A rabbi is here. He climbs up a few makeshift wooden steps to a makeshift pulpit. He painfully says, "Please everyone, let us pray together, let us say *Kaddish*, let us pray for so many who are no longer with us." This is our holiday of *Shavuot*; today we offer prayers for the dead.

The man next to me takes out a worn handkerchief from his pocket, wipes his eyes and blows his nose. His wife, who sits next to him, reaches for his bruised hand. The rabbi begins to speak as the murmur around him turns into identifiable words — words that are supposed to make us feel alive. At first, I say these words with everyone and then I think, 'What are we doing here? We are giving thanks to God for what he did to us?'

SIXTEEN

Henry stayed in Riga until the Russians came.
He cut off the toe on his left foot. He would not go
into the next forest.

—Inge

I AM STILL HOLDING Inge's hand when we walk outside. Her fingers are so slim and she is so frail. The Nazis took her body. I look down at her hand and then look at my hand. *Ja*, the Nazis took our engagement rings.

Ah, it all comes back to me now. That cold, rainy day in Neuendorf when Inge and I ran through the woods looking for shelter as the rain pelted us and soaked our clothes, our shoes, ourselves. There in the slight opening between the trees we found that little wooden shed. We found comfort. We found each other. I remember the look on her face when I reached into my damp pant pocket, opened my clenched hand, and offered her my heart. I put one metal band on her finger. She took the other and placed it on my finger. It was there in that little damp shack that we promised to come together after, after... here in Berlin.

Here, we walk the streets of Berlin. Maybe, if we are lucky, we would find someone from before. Then, I see him. I cannot remember his name anymore. No matter, he is yet another person still alive. He pushes a baby carriage as he walks next to a stately blond woman. I raise my arm for him to see me. "Over here, over here," I motion for him to look this way. "I am Gerd Bocian. Do you remember me? We went to school together." He looks at me and then nods to Inge. "Gerd — Gerd, it is you! I do remember you. My God, it is so good to see you!" He points to his lady friend and tells me, "This wonderful gentile German lady took me into her home where I remained in hiding... She was pregnant. She saved my life."

Inge is still so quiet with me. I am used to her smile, her vibrant laughter. I am sure that will come back in time. *Oy, oy,* she has been through so much. To think, Inge was only nineteen in Neuendorf when she was put on that transport. To think, all she has endured in her twenty-two years on this soil. I think, it is too much for one person to endure. My mind does this. I cannot keep from worrying about her. But, I walk on and take her hand once more. I like Inge's hand in mine. *Ja,* always her hand should be in mine.

We come to an edge in the roadway. Large rocks and stones have fallen in our way. We have to step carefully, or we will slip. Inge stops walking. Her face tells me she remembers something. She tugs my hand and quietly says, "Gerd, I want to know about my brother." Of course, my friend, the man we just spoke to must remind her of Henry, her only brother, who stayed in the house of their aunt, their mother's sister, when Inge came to Neuendorf.

Of course, now I understand why Inge listens every

night for an hour to a radio program, where people call in and give names of lost relatives. We walk some more, and we come to a familiar building around the corner. We go inside this radio station, and we sit on the wooden chairs along the wall. Soon it will be Inge's turn to speak.

Inge pulls the microphone in front of her. She takes a deep breath and lets the air out slowly. She clears her throat and says, "Henry, this is Inge, can you hear me Henry? It's me, Inge. I am in Berlin."

SEVENTEEN

*I wanted to forget. I just couldn't talk about it. I
never gave up. If you had no reason to live, you
were finished.*

—*Inge*

WE LIVE WITH MY FAMILY in my parents' apartment all summer. Inge remains mostly silent. When she looks out of our window, she seems to stare into the black hole that used to be Berlin. *Ja*, I am a bit more comfortable now that I know the four great powers — the United States, Great Britain, France, and the Soviet Union have come to help. My Berlin is divided into four parts, with these four powerful countries leading the way to our salvation. Yet, the buildings, the houses, the shops are still in rubble. This is what Inge sees when she looks out of the window.

"Come, Inge," I say. "Come outside with me. We will go for a walk. We will walk in these streets I still love, even after all that have been done to us."

Inge quietly puts on a gray cotton sweater over her simple cotton dress, which still hangs loosely on her small frame. I remember when I first saw her after she came back to me; she was skin and bones. I think she weighed only eighty pounds. I remember Inge telling me one day, "Gerd, how can you look at me? I am so skinny. You know, when I was there I think I could have weighed only sixty or seventy pounds. Now, I am not much better."

I am lucky that Inge confides in me. "Gerd, I am happy to live with your family all this time. They are so good to me, and I don't say nothing. I don't do nothing. What can I do? I am still so weak, and my hair is still growing back. I am still ashamed. In the camp, I always wore a scarf — my hair had no sunlight to grow. Even now, I can't look at myself in the mirror. I think I still look like a monkey."

I do not know what to say. The tears in my eyes cloud my thoughts. So, I take her by the hand and lead her out of our door.

We step lightly on the broken bricks, chipped rocks, piles of soot and dust that makes up this Berlin. The roar of machines pushing pieces of buildings into piles makes us shudder. Still, we walk. This reminds me of that day in Neuendorf when I knocked at Inge's door to ask her to come for that walk. I had a purpose that day, too. Today it is not raining. The summer sun tries to come out and casts a few shadows upon the buildings, upon the ground, upon us. Here is a broken metal bench with enough room for us to make ourselves comfortable.

This time, I don't have the metal bands in my pocket when I turn to Inge and ask, "Will you marry me, Inge? Will you marry me?"

Inge slowly turns toward me and places her frail hand in mine. It takes her a little while before she answers me. "Gerd, when we were in Neuendorf, we made each other a promise. If we survived, we would come back to Berlin. I found you, and you found me. I know why we stayed alive. I know I want to marry you. Yes, Gerd, yes."

The summer breezes turn into fall's colder days. My parents' apartment is filled with the joy and wonder of an approaching wedding. Everyone is so good to us—I could hardly believe it. And, Inge's beautiful brown eyes again sparkle. She is chattering again, just like when she walked each morning and talked with her three friends in Neuedorf. The war could not take everything.

I am beside myself with pride. I go to my father, who stands alone at the window. This is the man who has guided me my whole life. This is the man who taught me to be a man. We look into each others' eyes and without saying a word, I know what he is thinking.

We all stay up very late that evening. No one wants to go to bed. No one wants to part from each other. This is our last night together as this family. Tomorrow we will have one more person in our family. This is good. This is so very good.

In the presence of my sisters, my parents, my Neuendorf friends, and one man who survived Theresienstadt with me and who traveled back to Berlin with me, we gather together to mark this special day. Unbelieably, there is a knock on the door. A tall man stands there offering us a telegram sent by Inge's parents, who live in the United States. We are so overcome, we ask him to join the celebration.

My mother has found a beautiful lace tablecloth. Our table is set with crystal dishes and bowls; even a tall vase is filled with clusters of flowers. Two tall candelabras offer a quiet glow. An American chaplain has provided the cakes and the food. I am not afraid to partake.

Inge is beautiful in a dark-blue woolen wedding suit, borrowed from a neighbor. She wears my sister's navy suede shoes. A lace *mantilla*, once worn by a school friend, is Inge's wedding veil. The lace is placed just so that the center part in her brown hair shines just as Inge shines. My friend, Kurt Messerschmidt, has loaned me his black suit, black bow tie, and black shoes. A shiny black top hat sits on my head. Everything is borrowed. In my pocket, I have carefully folded a white handkerchief. On my lapel, Inge has pinned a floral boutonniere. I could not be happier.

So it is, on the 25th of November 1945, with this American chaplain dressed in Army formal attire, Inge and I stand side by side in my parents' apartment, under a lace *chuppa*—a lace tablecloth canopy held above our heads by four men.

We take our marriage vows.

Eighteen

We got a farm. It belongs to a Communist. We
work this farm. Now it is our farm.

—Gerd

WE ARE TWO PEOPLE that have become one. Inge
and I are married; she is no longer Inge Franke.
Together, we are Bocian.

Together we are strong, just like the story my father told
me so long ago about his Polish surname: Bocian, which
means 'stork.' My parents made their home in that strong
apartment building built near a stork's nest. Their synagogue
also was near this nest. With their religion and this image of
the storks flying in and out of their nest, it made sense that
if a stork could build a strong home and produce strong off-
spring, then my father believed he, too, would bring together
a strong family. *Ja,* Inge and I share a very good name.

Together we make our new life. A few months before
our wedding, a man by the name of Wredenhagen contacts

me. He owns a farm not far from Berlin in a little town called Breddin. Only Jewish people live in this town. Inge knows the wife from Auschwitz. The husband was also in a camp, because he is a Communist.

The man finds me and tells me, "Mr. Bocian, I need help on this farm. I need someone to oversee this farm." Without missing a beat, I answer, "Of course, I am eager to work. Before the war, I was in Neuendorf, an agricultural farm not far from here. I know how to plow the fields, plant and tend to vegetables. I know how to take care of horses, chickens and cows. I know how to oversee this farm. I am happy to take this job." I am the man he chooses. I am lucky. *Ja*, I am lucky in these difficult times to have this important job.

I go every day to this farm. A friend has a truck and sometimes I could ride with him. I get up sometimes before the sun rises to start walking in the streets of Berlin. I step around the dirty sandy piles of rubble so many times. Pebbles lodge in my shoes. I have another pair of shoes, which I tie together with the laces and sling them over my shoulder, with one shoe dangling in front, one shoe in back. Day after day, this is my life. But, it is a good life. Once again, I can say I am a proud man.

So, it is with tears in our eyes, Inge and I pack our meager belongings in makeshift cardboard suitcases we tie with rope. I go to my father and say, "Papa, it is so hard for me to leave you. You have been so good to me and now to Inge. But, this is something I must do." My father takes my hands in his and offers, "Gerd, Gerd, my boy, I love you with all my heart. I know you will make this farm prosper. Inge will, too." He calls Inge over and grasps her close to his chest. Inge trembles with love.

My parents and my sisters just stand silently and watch us take our newly found lives away from them.

Our marriage begins on this farm. The brick and concrete farmhouse is sturdy and welcoming. This man employs twelve Jewish workers, two cleaning girls and one cook. Inge is in heaven. I listen each morning as she gives formal instructions. "It is Monday, the beginning of our work week. I won't make the work difficult for you, but I demand perfection." Each cleaning girl is handed a list. It will take the whole week to do everything. Inge is at home.

The twelve men meet me at 5 AM every morning to begin our work. I work alongside them to ensure everything is done right. I love farming. I, too, am a perfectionist.

The weather changes as the German autumn brings damp, cold days, rainy days, snowy days. Winter moves in with fierce winds and more snow. This time, Inge and I do not live in barracks. We have warm wool blankets and plenty of food. We sit at a linen-covered table. Our dishes are not tin bowls. We don't have to hide our food, and no one steals from us.

We share this house with the owners, who live upstairs. We are downstairs away from the sounds of the help. Then, in the middle of one wintry night, we hear noises coming from above: sounds of furniture shifting, drawers opening and closing and loud voices we have never heard before. We see bright lights shine into the downstairs front windows. A war criminal, this German prisoner of war, held by the French, is found. He is found. We hear pounding footsteps on the stairs. We look out the window and see him and his wife climb into his big limousine driven by his chauffeur and drive off in the middle of the night. I cannot believe it.

While we eat our breakfast in the morning, I look up and see a piece of paper sticking out of the rafters above our table. I climb up and exclaim to Inge, "Look, look, what I have found. Here is a letter written by Mr. Wredenhagen.

He brags to his wife about his clandestine military work."
We always felt he was a crook. This confirms it. Still, we
need this farm. We remain on our farm.

We are here for another six months. The German weather turns warm, the fields are fresh from the winter snow,
the soil in our garden is being turned, and new seeds are
planted. One morning, I see an unfamiliar motor car approaching our house. Out comes an official-looking man,
who walks directly to me and says, "We implore you, Mr.
Bocian, to come to the Communist Party. We are prepared
to make you an offer you cannot refuse." He hands me the
papers but doesn't wait for me to read them. He gets back
into his car and drives away.

Inge comes up to me and with her knowing brown eyes,
says, "Gerd, we've seen enough."

This farm is no longer our safe home. We pack our belongings and we leave at midnight without looking back.

NINETEEN

*I'll never forget the day we go to the boat. I could
leave Germany behind.*

—Inge

Ja, WE STOLE OUT just after midnight that precarious
night. I thought Inge would be upset, but she showed
me how determined she could be. The farm was a wonderful place for us, as it reminded me of Neuendorf and
our good days. I have learned that I can do anything. Perhaps we will find something even better.

We are back in Berlin, again back to my parents'
apartment.

"Gerd, Inge… Is something wrong?" my father loudly
asks as he opens his front door and sees us in the hallway.

I explain, "Papa, we had no time to send you a message.
The farm was our home, we thought, until suddenly the
communist owner was taken away. We found a note he had

written to his wife, telling of his clandestine efforts during the war. We stayed on the farm as long as we could. We knew we had to leave one day. Now, we are back home with you and our family."

I do not know what else to say. Of course, we are welcome; anytime we would be welcome. My mother and sisters listen to our whole story. They are numb. "A glass of tea, Gerd? Maybe cookies, Inge?" my mother asks. She stands up, smoothes her housedress and does not wait for our answer. I watch her walk slowly into the kitchen. She is more bent over after all these months. Life has been so hard on her. I am glad we are home.

Our days are filled with mundane tasks. Sometimes, we help my father sweep and push the rubble away from the front of the building. Sometimes, Inge and I take a walk. Up and down the dirt-filled streets we walk, always looking for someone we might know. So many people are doing the same thing. We are all looking for something. What?

We are living here three months when I see Inge is keeping to herself again. She is not like that person who ran our farm. One gray morning Inge comes to me and says, "Gerd, I am only a little happy living here. I don't do anything. I don't know what I should do." Her round brown eyes plead for an answer, when she continues, "I am still so skinny, and I feel weak. My hair is still growing back. I always wore the scarf in the camp — I feel funny wearing it here. My hair has no sunlight. I still can't look at myself in the mirror. I still feel like I look like a monkey." *Oy*, why didn't I know Inge still feels this way?

Inge takes a breath before she continues. "Gerd, do you remember when I told you about our march from the camp, and this girl and I were in this little town, and we slept in a kindergarten? I have to tell you more. That British soldier we talked to — I wrote a letter to my parents and gave it to him to mail. The soldier said he would send it to America through the Jewish Council of Women. It was addressed to Solomon Franke, Brooklyn. I told them everything."

We sit together on the living room sofa. Inge's whole story comes back to me. I remember everything like it just happened. The four-page letter is embedded in my mind, and now the rest of her story sits in my head next to the part of my brain that keeps throbbing.

We stay with my family a couple more weeks. It is not easy anymore for Inge to be here. Every day she tells me, "Gerd, I miss my parents. I want to go to America."

So, it is with dread in my heart and with a longing to begin anew, Inge and I start out one early morning to the center of Berlin, where we find the headquarters of the American Jewish Joint Distribution Committee. I am confident they will help us. We could get German money because we were in the concentration camps. My father, too, has some money left. With a full heart, he offers some to us.

Again we must pack our clothes and possessions. We use the cardboard boxes my mother offers to us. We tie them with rough cord and leave a little cord handle to put our hands through. It is easy for me to carry these boxes, but I worry about Inge, already pregnant a few months. *Ja*, Inge is pregnant—already I am proud!

We are part of a large group of Jews, who are taken by the American Jewish Joint Distribution Committee to Hamburg. We are a little bit frightened to again be with so many people grouped together. We stay in a nice place in Hamburg for a few days. The morning we go to the boat, Inge calls out to me, "Gerd, Gerd, do you see that man? That English soldier is standing next to our boat, and he is holding a whip! Gerd, he is holding a whip."

I hear people talking. They say there is still trouble in Germany; there is still trouble with anti-Semitic people here. I look up one more time to that God.

This boat, this huge Marine Flasher called the *Liberty Ship*, is a 9,000-ton troop transport. *Oy*, it is so large, I can hardly believe it. We are separated. Inge and I, the men and women are not allowed to sleep together. We sleep in hammocks, one on top of another, for ten days. Inge is so small. We are lucky that her pregnancy does not show. The rocky seas and crashing waves don't disturb her. I am thankful.

I am thankful, too, when we land in America. It is June 18, 1946. It is Inge's father's birthday.

TWENTY

*I was sixteen years old when the war started.
Now, I am twenty two. I haven't seen my
parents in six years.*

—Inge

THE JOURNEY TAKES only ten days, but it seems
much longer. I walk around all these people every day to go and see Inge. "Gerd, do you know
how I feel?" she asks." I feel like I am back on that transport from Neuendorf. I sleep on this rope hammock, but
it is no better than the little wooden board I called my
bed when I was in the camp. I am embarrassed to be telling you this."

I take Inge in my outstretched arms and pull her close.
"We will be there soon, Inge; we will be home soon."

We enter the harbor on a wet, windy New York day.
New York. *Ja*, we have traveled to America. Together, Inge
and I have traveled to this place they call Ellis Island. It

floats in the middle of blue water, like the water is welcoming us home.

It takes so long to get off the boat. There are so many people, and so many people looking for just a few. Just like us. Our lives are still cramped. Inge and I take our cardboard suitcases and walk with pride down the ramp onto the cold, gray concrete floor below. Inge puts her hand over her eyes and rests it on her forehead, like she is looking far, far away, to find someone so close.

"Mama, Mama, I am here, we are here..." Inge's words trail off as she puts her suitcase on the floor. Her mother sees her almost at the same instant, and I watch as they run to each other. They hold on to each other, like they are holding on to their lives. *Ja*, what I am thinking is probably true. I follow, but I want them to have time together first. "Inge... Inge... my daughter... my daughter..." I watch as I see their bodies tremble.

Inge motions to me. "Gerd, come over here, Gerd, come meet my family."

All of her family has not come. Inge's aunt, her mother's sister, is standing on one side, but Inge doesn't see her father. Her mother says, "Inge, your father has not been well. When we received your letter, your father collapsed. He had a heart attack. Then about four months later, he had another attack. Oh, Inge, he is not well. He does not have the strength to come up here. He could not climb all this way."

I have never felt such emotion, even when I came back to Berlin. We all just stand in our little circle. No one says a word, until Inge turns to me and says, "Gerd, I have to go to the toilet."

Just like that she begins to walk down the sloped pavement to an area below. I see her as she sees someone, an older man, sitting on a metal bench. He stands when he sees her, takes off his hat and holds it in front of him in his two hands.

"Is that you, Inge?"

"Papa?"

TWENTY ONE

Gerd

I CANNOT KEEP THIS to myself any longer. There is an image in my mind I never will be able to erase, no matter how long I live.

During the two years in camp Theresienstadt, witnessing death, murder, hangings, and torture, I do not remember ever shedding any tears, with the exception of one night, standing by helpless, desperate, paralyzed with fear, wanting to help and I could not. There were eight of us boys, that rainy winter night, three months before the war ended, when the SS told us to go to the train station and empty the cattle cars while they chased people out. These were French women and children getting off that train. I see them running, running, running in every direction..

Why was I and these few boys at this time and place all together? Why? I ask myself this question over and over again. It doesn't leave my mind and my heart.

I see this woman, running, running with her little child, Shulamit, in her arms. Then I hear the beast, the SS man, Heindl; he was the worst. He was the worst. He yells at them, "*Halt, halt...*" And, I see him shoot them. And I see him shoot them. It was a minute or two; that is all it took.

Little Shulamit, so beautiful, so young, so innocent, died in front of my eyes, together with the Jewish God I had grown up to believe in... to fear... to trust. Hitler killed them both. This image is in front of me for thirty five years after the war, every night when I try to fall asleep. *Ja*, it was thirty-five years, and my first granddaughter was born. My little Lisa, my daughter's child, is born. Some of the pain that I carry is lessened; she makes it easier for me. Falling asleep each night has almost stopped being a nightmare.

In the Jewish religion, we name our newborns after a family member who is deceased. When Lisa was born, my daughter, Debbie, named Lisa for Inge's father, Solomon Franke. His Hebrew name was Schlomo. Lisa's Hebrew name, the name for a girl... is Shulamit.

I never told my children the story of my Shulamit.

I remember when Lisa was four, and I was taking care of her and her new little sister, Jill. I had my arms around Lisa, sitting with her on the living room sofa in her house, and I began to cry.

"Poppy, I look into your face, and your cheeks are all wet. Poppy, I want to know why you are crying," my little Lisa asks.

"Because we Jews do not only cry when we are sad," I tell her. "Sometimes, we cry when we are happy. Lisa, I am happy you are here with me today." I cannot tell her I am crying because of Shulamit. I do tell her how much we love her and how our hearts grow bigger with each new grand-child. This is true.

Heindl was hanged in 1948. The noose around his neck does not give me any relief, any satisfaction, or whatever; it makes me relive that winter night when he murdered Shulamit.

Today, Hitler's shadow still follows me some sixty years after the Holocaust. When I go to *shul* for Friday night services or on the holiday of Purim, I see the little children walking up to the *bima* — the raised carpeted plat-form where the rabbi stands — to get their candy and their blessing from our rabbi, and I wonder, why do I go? Why do I go? I have mixed feelings. Can I enjoy Purim, really? With one laughing and one tearing eye, I go. I go.

It is still so hard for me; it is hard for me to let go of my little Shulamit. She is buried in my mind, my memo-ries, my deepest dreams. For the sake of all Jewish children murdered during the tragic Jewish history, for the sake of all humanity and civilization, I am still crying.

AUTHOR'S NOTE

The Florida sun continues to shine through the top of the swaying palm tree. The green palm fronds cast eerie shadows on the pristine white walls inside this concrete condominium. Memories of grotesquely shaped German trees in that dense gray sky still don't go away. The Bocians' apartment, decorated in black and white, is still home for Inge and Jerry (Gerd) who celebrated sixty-five years together.

We spent eighteen months together in this apartment. The tape-recorded conversations contained each word Jerry and Inge spoke. Each sentence I wrote brought me to a closer understanding about how these two exceptional people survived a horrific, tumultuous ordeal.

The first time I rang their doorbell was on a Wednesday afternoon, at 2:00 pm, April 20. Hitler's birthday. At the time, I didn't know it was Hitler's birthday; Inge told me.

Not long ago, Jerry Bocian, now in his late eighties, needed medical attention. On one of his office visits to my husband, Dr. Gary Krulik, an orthopedic surgeon, he had tucked under his arm an old newspaper clipping and a black-and-white photo copy of a gravestone. The story and the photo was about a Polish rabbi by the name of Kupfersztoch, known as The Warsaw Rav, who lived in the same apartment house on the same floor, next to Jerry's parents' apartment in the center of Berlin. Jerry carries with him a picture of this strong, distinguished man, who was instrumental in saving his own life, his parents' and his sisters' lives and the lives of hundreds of Jews during Hitler's bloody war.

He handed the paper and photo to my husband and said, "I am a Holocaust survivor. My wife, Inge, is a Holocaust survivor. We would like our story told."

Jerry never told me the reason he brought those papers or the reason why he told this story to my husband. Perhaps, sixty years after his incarceration, it was time to put it all in print.

Perhaps it was a wish to get rid of his constant migraine headaches. He did tell me that he suffered from such headaches from the time he was seven years old. He began taking pain pills when he was seventeen. He said, "I was so used to taking painkillers. But, when I came to Neuendorf, I couldn't take the pills anymore. For two weeks I was in shock. The doctor took me off aspirin a little at a time. For a while I had rebound headaches and then after a while, nothing. Only after the camps, after Theresienstadt, the headaches came back."

So it began. At least once or twice a month, I arrived at 2:00 PM on Wednesday afternoons for eighteen months. We sat at their round breakfast table covered in a white tablecloth delicately embroidered with colorful designs. Inge said she did not embroider the cloth, but she has favorite clothes she puts on this table. I sat with my back to the window where I could see through their kitchen to the black-and-white family room and out the window to that tall palm tree beyond. Jerry sat always on my left, ready with a folder filled with notes and his remembrances of this history. Inge sat across from me, her arms on the table,

# # #

her hands clasped in front. Both arms still shake. She is so troubled with the constant tremors. Inge said, "Never in Neuendorf. Never in Auschwitz did my arms shake. It only happened when we came to America, when I saw my parents again."

A portable tape recorder was centered on top of the table between Inge and Jerry. We talked for more than an hour each visit. Along with the papers came more and more memories. They offered me a glass of water or a cup of hot tea or some of Inge's home-baked ruggelah pastry. They showed me Inge's framed needlepoint collection hanging on the kitchen wall. They walked with me into the living room to see family photos displayed on shelves.

One Wednesday afternoon as we completed our session, Inge, who was usually more quiet than Gerd, once again offered me tea. Then she told me, "You know, when I was in Auschwitz, all we had to eat was foul-smelling soup. Every day the guards dipped a dirty ladle into this oversized vat of this 'soup.' I put my dirty metal bowl out in front of me. Some of the liquid spilled from the bowl and made my hands smell. All I ever wanted was a glass of hot water with lemon. Just a glass of hot water with lemon. I said this to Gerd when we were together in Berlin. I thought that was what I wanted. Once I came home and we lived with my parents in Brooklyn, I never again asked for that glass of hot lemon water." Inge looked directly at me. She was satisfied that now I knew this, too.

With each session, from their past came the present. Jerry's parents remained in Berlin and were buried there. From time to time, Jerry and Inge traveled back to see his parents, who still lived in the same apartment house—the building with the outer iron gate, the building that also housed the Rav, the building that had two German policemen with submachine guns protecting this famous rabbi.

As it turned out, these policemen were Jerry's parents' protectors, too.

When we sat at their round glass table and when Inge offered me a glass of water or some home-made pastry, she looked content. Only one time she placed her arms upon this table, clasped her hands together, turned to me and offered, "I never would have gone back to Germany if Gerd's parents weren't still living there."

Rabbi Kupfersztoch died of natural causes in his apartment on March 2, 1940. He was buried two days later on March 4, 1940, in the Jewish Cemetery, Adass Jisroel.

Jerry and Inge made a memorable trip to Germany in 1988, on the 50th anniversary of *Kristallnacht*. First, they made a journey to the rabbi's grave in Berlin. Then, they traveled once again to Neuendorf. These were both emotional trips, which remain embedded in their minds and hearts.

The original building in Neuendorf burned to the ground after the war and was rebuilt by the Communists. A commemorative plaque is still visible on the side of the main building. In essence, it reads:

> *On this farm, Neuendorf, there existed between 1940 and 1943 an Agricultural School for Jews, that these people could have a chance to emigrate. In fact, these people were sent away to Death Camps to settle the Jewish situation. With the last transport on April 20, 1943, there was also a group of children with the Jewish teacher, Clara Grumwald, who was sent to gas chambers in Auschwitz. We remember them with honor, November 9, 1988. The 50th year of Kristallnacht.*

I remember the absolute silence in the apartment after these words were spoken.

Inge, who was usually quiet during these tapings unless I prodded her with a direct question, told me about an event she clearly recalls: an emotional event in 1941 between herself and Jerry, a sensitive poem she wrote to him when they were still together in Neuendorf:

> *I do not write a long and fancy poem*
> *I plead with you, very simple, do not forget me*
> *In remembrance of our beautiful time in Neuendorf.*

Inge never liked her German name, Ingeborg, and never liked Jerry's German name, Gerhard. She still calls him Gerd.

Like her husband, Inge is proud of her married name and perhaps the strength it has continued to give her. Inge always told me, "I was lucky." She was lucky all the days in Auschwitz and even more lucky when, at the age of twenty-two, she was the first Holocaust survivor to give birth to a baby in the United States. The baby boy, born on October 13, 1946, who also survived that ocean crossing on the *Liberty Ship,* came just four months after his mother landed in America.

There was a newspaper article announcing the birth, but it mistakenly printed that the Nazis attempted to sterilize her. This never happened, Inge said. There is something that did happen when her children — a daughter came later — were young and in elementary school. They had never spoken of their parents being in concentration camps. In fact, when each child's teacher asked their class if anyone knew of survivors, neither child spoke. Inge and Jerry said they learned their children didn't fully understand what had happened during the war and thought the number tattooed on their mother's arm was a phone number. Inge and Jerry went to the school to talk with the principal. It took this episode for Inge to have the tattoo removed. She said, "Just because Hitler put it there, didn't mean I had to keep it there."

What they did keep, along with the memories, are two songs. The first is the German torch song, *Lili Marlene*, the tune they each heard in different places during the war, and hoped the other was hearing it, too. When they talk about this song, they both still smile.

The French song, *J'attendrai*, is part of their lives today. The song's story is a love ballad of two people during the war, who wait for one another every day and every night. Their simultaneous pain waiting for each other's return is both pathetic and lovely. Like the song, Gerd waits for Inge to come to his parents' apartment door. The wall clock ticks too many hours. Her footsteps are not heard. Yet, for Gerd, the wind outside brings formative sounds, and he rushes to find her like the wind.

From their past, Jerry and Inge have created a fine present. In their apartment today, in a small hallway with the ceiling far above their heads, hangs a bronze *shabbas* lamp. So many years ago, this lamp hung in Inge's parents' Brooklyn apartment, and now here.

The lamp is yet one more Holocaust survivor.

PHOTOGRAPHS

PHOTOGRAPHS BY DAVID THOMASON, PH.D.

From Auschwitz, Poland and Terezin, Czechoslovakia

The electric fence at Auschwitz, as seen in 2008.

The Nazi death camp at Birkenau (Auschwitz II).

View of the Birkenau concentration camp. The grounds, the buildings, the electric fence.

The tracks at Birkenau.

The courtyard between two brick buildings at Auschwitz. The iron window bars and wooden window closures kept Jews in, not out.

The sleeping building at Auschwitz. Men and women were separated.

Shadows creep along the building of lost lives at Auschwitz.

The toilets at Auschwitz. Inge hid precious items on the beams above.

The entrance to Theresienstadt (Terezin), the model ghetto.

The buildings at Theresienstadt (Terezin).

Sleeping quarters at Theresienstadt (Terezin).

Block A building at Theresienstadt, (Terezin).

This painted yellow building housed the Guards and SS Officers at Theresienstadt, (Terezin).

View of the large, walled city, Theresienstadt (Terezin), the model ghetto.

Another, closer, view of the entrance to Theresienstadt. The moat around the old city of Terezin that was the model ghetto, while the prison was only a few kilometers away. In the distance is the bridge into the city and the city gate. The reflection in the mirror is of two houses behind the photographer.

ACKNOWLEDGMENTS

Writing this book was both a loving and formidable task. It could not have been accomplished without the generosity and time given to me by people who became instrumental as I brought to life this horrific time in history.

My continued gratitude and sincere thanks go to:

Lucille Gang Shulklapper: extraordinary writer, poet, dear friend, whose timely advice and insight into the world of words helped make these pages come alive.

Joyce Sweeney: a superb mentor and writing coach, whose editorial expertise gave credence and meaning to each chapter. To the writers and authors in Joyce Sweeney's Thursday Night Writers' Group, my thanks for your approval and timely suggestions for each chapter read aloud. You provided the threads that bound this book together.

Helen Rubens: lifelong friend, advance reader, and outstanding advisor, helped to give strong meaning to the word, "Holocaust."

Tracy Krulik: my daughter, whose post-graduate musical studies included a course in the music of Theresienstadt. Thank you for providing information for the DVD, "Theresienstadt: Gateway to Auschwitz-Recollections from Childhood." The pictures provided a closer connection to this concentration camp; they continue to haunt.

Sheila and Paul Golden, thank you for your personal attention and dedicated research for the song, *J'attendrai*.

And, thanks to Judy and Bruce Borich Middle River Press, whose careful attention to detail brought this whole project together.